MARY BERRY'S
FAVOURITE
RECIPES

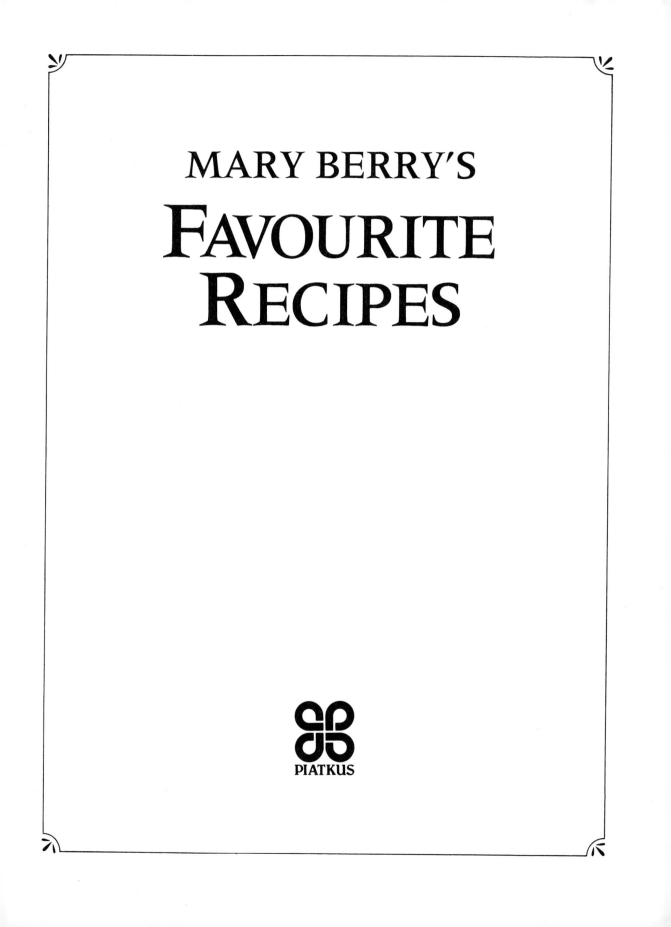

PIATKUS

© 1988 by Mary Berry

First published in Great Britain in 1988 by
Judy Piatkus (Publishers) Limited,
5 Windmill Street, London W1P 1HF

British Library Cataloguing in Publication Data

Berry, Mary, *1935–*
    Mary Berry's favourite recipes.
    1. Food. Recipes.
    I. Title
    641.5

ISBN 0–86188–766–2

Designed and illustrated by Paul Saunders
Photographs facing pages 33, 64, 96, 97, 128, 160
and 225 by Tim Imrie; photograph facing page 65 by
British Meat; other photographs by John Lee.

Phototypeset in 11/12pt Linotron Imprint by
Phoenix Photosetting, Chatham
Printed and bound in Great Britain at
The Bath Press, Avon

CONTENTS

INTRODUCTION

The recipes in this book all have one thing in common – they have all been asked for by friends, viewers and readers time and time again. Some have appeared in other books, some in magazines. I have made a few small alterations here and there to bring them more into line with today's tastes and the growing interest in healthy eating, but essentially they remain the same well-loved recipes.

Families these days eat fewer roasts and a little less red meat, and I have therefore included plenty of recipes for chicken along with the many favourite beef, lamb and pork recipes. In the fish chapter I have included dishes for every occasion, from a simple family lunch to an elegant buffet supper.

Other changes in the way we eat now are reflected in the wide selection of appetisers I have included, and a number of recipes throughout the book have an 'international' flavour. Previously hard-to-come-by ingredients are becoming more widely available every day, and there is more opportunity than ever for experimenting with dishes your family may have enjoyed when on holiday or eating out.

Having said all that, some things just don't change – among them the popularity of home-baked puddings and cakes. These perennial favourites are well represented, as are cold desserts for special occasions, and teabreads, biscuits and scones to provide the basis for a traditional teatime spread.

Also thoroughly traditional is the chapter on Christmas cookery. Everything you need for Christmas day is included there, so you have all the recipes together when you want them. For entertaining of a different kind, I have included a number of ideas for finger food to nibble with drinks.

Cooking is for most of us something that happens each day. I do hope this book will help to make it a more enjoyable task. There are lots of recipes here to bring forth oohs and aahs from all the family.

Equipment

With a family to cook for, I wouldn't be without my food processor. A more robust and versatile machine than a blender, it works quite differently too. A blender works best when the ingredients are fairly liquid; a processor is most efficient when most of the liquid is drained off first or the mixture is fairly dry. As well as making super-smooth purées, processors are fast and efficient at such tasks as chopping nuts, making breadcrumbs and mincing meat. Give a thought, too, to the order in which you process ingredients – don't start off with the garlic!

Freezers also simplify life enormously. Few cooks have a cold larder these days but most have at least a small freezer, so use it for storing extra supplies of basic ingredients. Once upon a time, the idea was to cook and freeze huge batches of food, but we have all grown more accustomed to freezers now. If you are having steak and kidney pie today, make an extra one for the freezer by all means, but schedule it ahead for a particular occasion.

Although food will remain safe to eat for

ages in the freezer, it will deteriorate in flavour after a time so it makes sense not to stockpile it for too long. Remember, also, that anything whole freezes better than anything with exposed surfaces, so joints freeze better than cutlets, and cutlets freeze better than mince.

A microwave, too, is useful – as a part-cooker, for thawing things from the freezer and for odd jobs such as melting butter or warming bread rolls. It is also excellent for cooking fish, sauces and vegetables. However, while it is very efficient if you are cooking for just one or two, it is often slower than a conventional oven for larger quantities.

The young enjoy cooking with the microwave, and it is absolutely safe. It also comes into its own if you want to cook food ahead and then reheat it, say for a dinner party or if a member of the family will be arriving too late for a mealtime.

GOOD SOUPS

Home-made soups are much cheaper and better for you than cans and packets which tend to contain a lot of unnecessary additives. They freeze well, too, but don't add all the liquid called for in the recipe before you put them in the freezer – add the remainder when you thaw and reheat.

I very rarely cook at lunchtime, and a bowl of good home-made soup with crusty bread or rolls is a satisfying alternative to cold meat or sandwiches.

Carrot and Orange Soup

Use orange juice from a carton, the kind you have for breakfast and keep in the refrigerator. No need to add the cream if you like it less rich.

PREPARATION AND COOKING TIME: 20 minutes

2 oz (50 g) butter
8 oz (225 g) onion, finely chopped
2 lb (900 g) carrots, sliced
1 pint (600 ml) orange juice
salt
freshly ground black pepper
1 pint (600 ml) good chicken stock
¼ pint (150 ml) double cream
2 tablespoons snipped chives

Heat the butter in a pan and fry the onion until soft but not brown, then tip into a processor. Cook the carrots in boiling salted water for about 15 minutes until just tender then drain and add to the onion. Process to a purée, then add the orange juice and seasoning through the funnel of the processor. Blend in the stock.

Stir in the cream and chives just before serving, either very cold or piping hot.

SERVES 8

Courgette Soup

In midsummer courgettes are most plentiful and at their best. Grate the courgettes in a processor for speed.

PREPARATION AND COOKING TIME: 35 minutes

2 oz (50 g) butter
1 small onion, finely chopped
1½ lb (675 g) courgettes, coarsely grated
1½ oz (40 g) flour
¾ pint (450 ml) good chicken stock
¾ pint (450 ml) milk
a little grated nutmeg
salt
freshly ground black pepper

Melt the butter in a large pan and quickly sauté the onion for about 5 minutes until golden brown, then add the courgettes and fry until they begin to soften. Stir in the flour and cook for 2 minutes, then gradually blend in the stock and bring to the boil, stirring until thickened.

Stir in the milk, nutmeg and seasoning and bring the soup back to the boil. Cover and simmer gently for about 20 minutes, then taste and check seasoning.

Serve piping hot.

SERVES 6

Watercress Soup

Use the very best pieces of watercress for garnish or for a salad, and use stalks and less beautiful leaves in this delicious soup.

PREPARATION AND COOKING TIME: 30 minutes

2 bunches watercress
2 oz (50 g) butter
1 onion, peeled and sliced
12 oz (350 g) potatoes, peeled and sliced
1 pint (600 ml) good chicken stock
salt
freshly ground black pepper
¾ pint (450 ml) milk
¼ pint (150 ml) single cream

Wash the watercress but do not remove the stalks. Melt the butter in a pan and gently cook the onion and potato for 5 minutes without browning. Add the stock and seasoning, bring to the boil, then cover and simmer for about 15 minutes. Add the watercress and simmer for a further 10 minutes, then purée in a processor or blender.

Return the puréed soup to the pan, stir in the milk and heat through. Stir in the cream just before serving.

SERVES 6

Mild Curried Parsnip Soup

A really smashing soup, well worth making when parsnips are at their best and cheapest.

PREPARATION AND COOKING TIME: 35 minutes

3 oz (75 g) butter
4 oz (100 g) onion, chopped
1 lb (450 g) parsnips, cubed
1 fat clove garlic, crushed
1 oz (25 g) flour
1 rounded teaspoon curry powder
2 pints (1.2 litres) good beef stock
salt
freshly ground black pepper
¼ pint (150 ml) single cream
snipped chives

Melt the butter in a large pan, add the onion, parsnip and garlic, and fry gently for about 5 minutes. Stir in the flour and curry powder and cook for a minute, then blend in the stock and seasoning. Bring to the boil, stirring, then cover and simmer gently for about 20 minutes, until the parsnip is tender. Sieve the soup, or process in a processor or blender until smooth.

Reheat until piping hot, then taste and check seasoning. Stir in the cream just before serving, and sprinkle chives on top.

SERVES 6

Lentil Soup

Like most pulses, lentils are very high in food value.

PREPARATION AND COOKING TIME: 1¼ hours

8 oz (225 g) orange lentils
1 large onion, chopped
3 sticks celery, chopped
2 medium potatoes, diced
2 pints (1.2 litres) good chicken stock
salt
freshly ground black pepper

Rinse the lentils well under cold running water. Put all the ingredients in a large saucepan, bring to the boil and cover with a lid. Reduce the heat and simmer for about an hour, until the lentils are tender.

Allow the soup to cool slightly, then reduce to a purée in a processor or blender. Reheat the soup in a clean saucepan and serve very hot.

SERVES 6

Fast Tomato Soup

Make this soup in 15 minutes flat from ingredients that are usually in the home. If you have chives in the garden, add chopped chives before serving instead of parsley.

PREPARATION AND COOKING TIME: 15 minutes

1 oz (25 g) butter
1 small onion, finely chopped
1 oz (25 g) flour
½ pint (300 ml) water
2½ oz (62 g) can tomato purée
½ pint (300 ml) milk
1 teaspoon caster sugar
salt
freshly ground black pepper
grated Parmesan cheese
freshly chopped parsley

Melt the butter in a saucepan, add the onion and fry gently for about 5 minutes, or until soft but not coloured. Stir in the flour and cook for a minute, without colouring.

Draw the pan off the heat and gradually add the water and tomato purée. Stir until smooth, then return to the heat and bring to the boil, stirring until thickened. Add the milk, sugar and seasoning, stir until well blended and simmer gently for 7 minutes.

Taste and check seasoning. Pour the soup into bowls, sprinkle with cheese and parsley, and serve at once.

SERVES 2 to 3

Cucumber and Mint Soup

A wonderful soup. We usually have it hot but it is equally good cold.

PREPARATION AND COOKING TIME: 35 minutes

2 oz (50 g) butter
1 medium onion, chopped
2 large cucumbers, peeled and seeded
1½ oz (40 g) flour
1 pint (600 ml) light stock
8 sprigs mint
salt
freshly ground black pepper
½ pint (300 ml) milk
a little single cream

Heat the butter in a large pan, add the onion and sauté, covered, for about 15 minutes. Carefully dice a quarter of the cucumber and reserve for garnish; roughly chop the remainder and add to the pan with the onion. Sprinkle in the flour, then gradually blend in the stock and bring to the boil, stirring until thickened. Add six of the sprigs of mint and seasoning, and simmer for about 10 minutes.

Remove the mint and reduce the soup to a purée in a processor, then return it to the pan. Stir in the milk and the reserved cucumber and heat until piping hot. Taste and check seasoning, and stir in a little extra milk if the soup is on the thick side. Chop the remaining sprigs of mint and serve the soup with a swirl of cream and a sprinkling of mint.

SERVES 4 to 6

Gazpacho

A soup to make when tomatoes are really cheap in late summer. Be sure to choose ripe ones. Skin tomatoes by dropping them into boiling water till the skins burst, then quickly transfer them to cold water. The skins will slip off easily. This recipe can also be made using canned tomatoes.

PREPARATION AND COOKING TIME: 15 minutes
CHILLING TIME: 6 hours

2 lb (900 g) ripe tomatoes, skinned and sliced
1 large onion, sliced
2 fat cloves garlic, crushed
2 slices white bread, crusts removed
4 tablespoons white wine vinegar
5 tablespoons olive oil
1/2 pint (300 ml) good chicken stock
2 oz (50 g) green pepper, very finely diced
juice of 1/2 lemon
salt
freshly ground black pepper
diced cucumber and small bread croûtons to garnish

Put the tomatoes, onion, garlic, bread, vinegar, oil and stock in a processor or blender and process for a few seconds until the mixture is well blended. Turn the mixture into a bowl, then stir in the green pepper, lemon juice and seasoning. Chill for at least 6 hours.

Serve garnished with diced cucumber and bread croûtons.

SERVES 4 to 6

APPETISERS
AND PÂTÉS

Keep portions small, and vary your selection according to what is to follow. It sounds obvious, but if appetisers are to be appetising then hot ones should be really hot and cold ones really cold. Pâtés that are to be sliced must be thoroughly chilled before they are turned out, while those that are to be spread should be served at room temperature.

As well as being excellent first courses, many of these recipes make lovely light supper dishes too.

Palm Hearts au Gratin

Palm hearts are delicious and crunchy. Creamy white in colour, they look rather like the base of a leek.

PREPARATION AND COOKING TIME: 45 minutes

14 oz (425 g) can palm hearts
1½ oz (40 g) butter
1½ oz (40 g) flour
¾ pint (450 ml) milk
4 oz (100 g) Emmenthal cheese, grated
1 good teaspoon Dijon mustard
generous grating of nutmeg
salt
freshly ground black pepper

Heat the oven to 425°F/220°C/Gas Mark 7. Drain the palm hearts and throw away the liquid. Slice the palm hearts in half lengthways and then into three or four pieces.

Next, make a good white sauce. Heat the butter in a pan and add the flour; cook for a minute then gradually blend in the milk, stirring until smooth and thickened. Add two thirds of the cheese, the mustard, nutmeg, salt and pepper, then stir the palm hearts into the sauce. Taste and check seasoning.

Divide the mixture between six ramekin or individual soufflé dishes and sprinkle over the remaining cheese. Cook in the oven for 20 minutes until crispy brown on top.

SERVES 6

Garlic Mushrooms with Cream

You need really small, fresh, white button mushrooms for this dish, other-wise the creamy sauce will be grey.

PREPARATION AND COOKING TIME: 15 minutes

12 oz (350 g) small button mushrooms
1½ oz (40 g) butter
1 fat clove garlic, crushed
salt
freshly ground black pepper
¼ pint (150 ml) double cream

Wash the mushrooms and trim the ends off the stalks. Melt the butter in a large frying pan or saucepan, add the garlic and mushrooms and cook for 5 minutes.

Season well, stir in the cream and simmer gently for a further 5 minutes or until the mushrooms are tender. Divide between four ramekins or small dishes and serve hot.

SERVES 4

Individual Hot Cheese Soufflés

You can prepare these soufflés in advance and freeze them covered with clingfilm. Cook them when almost thawed, for a little longer than the time given in the recipe.

PREPARATION AND COOKING TIME: 40 minutes

1¹/₂ oz (40 g) butter
1¹/₂ oz (40 g) flour
¹/₂ pint (300 ml) milk
¹/₂ teaspoon made mustard
large pinch grated nutmeg
2 oz (50 g) Cheddar cheese, grated
2 oz (50 g) Parmesan cheese, grated
salt
freshly ground black pepper
3 large eggs, separated

Heat the oven to 350°F/180°C/Gas Mark 4. Butter six to eight ramekins, depending on the size, and dust with extra Parmesan cheese, if you like.

Melt the butter in a pan, then remove from the heat and blend in the flour. Return to a gentle heat and cook for a minute, stirring. Remove the pan from the heat again and add the milk a little at a time, stirring well so that no lumps form. Return to the heat and bring to the boil, stirring until thick and smooth, and cook for a minute. Remove the pan from the heat and beat in the mustard, nutmeg, cheeses and seasoning; when these are well blended, stir in the egg yolks one at a time.

Whisk the egg whites with a rotary or electric hand whisk just until peaks form and tip over when lifted on the whisk. Using a metal spoon, fold a table-spoon of the egg white into the sauce, then carefully fold in the remaining egg white, working the mixture as little as possible so that air is not knocked out. Divide between the ramekin dishes and run a teaspoon around the edge of each dish. Bake in the oven for about 20 minutes or until well risen and golden brown. Serve at once.

SERVES 6 to 8

Melon and Tomato in Mint Dressing

A lovely fresh first course. For how to skin tomatoes easily, see page 17.

PREPARATION TIME: 15 minutes
CHILLING TIME: 2 hours

1 honeydew or Galia melon
12 oz (350 g) firm tomatoes
1 cucumber
2 teaspoons mint jelly
1 tablespoon caster sugar
2 tablespoons wine vinegar
6 tablespoons corn or vegetable oil
salt
freshly ground black pepper
6 small sprigs fresh mint

Cut the melon in half and remove the seeds. Either scoop the melon flesh out using a melon baller, or peel the melon and cut the flesh into cubes.

Skin and quarter the tomatoes and remove the seeds (if the tomatoes are large, cut each quarter in half). Peel the cucumber and cut it into neat dice. Put the cucumber, melon and tomatoes in a large bowl and mix well together.

Melt the mint jelly in a saucepan with the sugar and vinegar, then remove from the heat and allow to cool. Mix in the oil and seasoning, then pour the dressing over the salad and toss well. Chill in a cool place. Taste and check seasoning, then serve in individual glasses, garnished with fresh mint.

SERVES 6

Salade Niçoise

This salad needs careful and gentle tossing, otherwise the egg and tuna will become too mixed in and lose their shape.

PREPARATION TIME: 10 minutes

3 tomatoes, skinned (page 17), quartered and seeded
½ cucumber, peeled and diced
8 oz (225 g) French beans, cooked and cut in short lengths
1 small green pepper, quartered, seeded and thinly sliced
½ mild Spanish onion, finely chopped
about 5 tablespoons French dressing (page 153)
1 cos lettuce, cut in 2 inch (5 cm) slices
7 oz (200 g) can tuna fish, drained and flaked
2 oz (50 g) can anchovy fillets, drained
2 oz (50 g) small black olives
2 hard-boiled eggs
coarsely chopped parsley

Put the tomatoes, cucumber, beans, green pepper and onion in a large bowl. Pour the French dressing over the vegetables and mix lightly.

Arrange the lettuce in the bottom of a salad bowl or serving dish, then spoon the vegetables over it. Arrange the tuna fish, anchovy fillets and black olives on top. Cut the hard-boiled eggs in halves lengthways and place on the salad. Sprinkle with parsley and serve at once.

SERVES 4

Buchanan Herrings

One of the most delicious and simple first courses. It's quite an unusual combination, the banana taking away the sharpness of the rollmop herrings. Serve with brown bread and butter.

PREPARATION TIME: 10 minutes

6 bananas
juice of 1 lemon
½ pint (300 ml) mayonnaise (page 152)
4 rollmop herrings
enough mixed green salad to cover eight plates
fresh parsley, dill or fennel

Peel the bananas, cut them in half lengthways, then slice them into a bowl. Pour the lemon juice over the bananas and mix together, then stir in the mayonnaise. Cut the rollmops into small, manageable pieces and stir into the mayonnaise.

Arrange the green salad over eight individual plates and divide the herring mixture between them. Decorate with parsley, dill or fennel.

SERVES 8

Scallops au Gratin

Scallops are best from October to April. If they are a bit expensive you could use just one scallop per person and add 4 oz (100 g) sliced button mushrooms, sautéed first in butter.

PREPARATION AND COOKING TIME: 30 minutes

8 scallops
8 tablespoons white wine
1 oz (25 g) butter
1 oz (25 g) flour
½ pint (300 ml) milk
2 to 3 oz (50 to 75 g) grated cheese
1 egg yolk
2 tablespoons cream or top of the milk

Remove the scallops from their shells, wash thoroughly and remove the beards and any black parts. Place them in a pan with the wine and simmer gently for 3 minutes.

Meanwhile, make the sauce. Melt the butter in a saucepan, blend in the flour and cook for a minute without browning. Slowly stir in the milk and bring to the boil, stirring until thickened.

Remove the scallops from the pan with a slotted spoon and boil the wine rapidly until it has reduced to 1 tablespoon. Stir this into the sauce with three quarters of the cheese and beat until smooth. Blend the egg yolk with the cream and add this to the sauce, then season to taste. Reheat but do not boil the sauce.

Place a little sauce into four scallop shells, then cut the scallops into pieces and lay them in the shells. Spoon over the remaining sauce and sprinkle the remaining cheese on top. Place the scallops under a moderate grill for about 5 minutes, until the cheese has melted and is golden brown and bubbling. Serve at once.

SERVES 4

Gravad Lax

A classic Scandinavian recipe for pickled fresh salmon, given to me by a great fishing expert. This speciality is appearing in top restaurants in Britain – no wonder, it tastes quite wonderful served with mustard dill sauce, brown bread and unsalted butter. It is not difficult to prepare – leave the salmon to marinate for up to 5 days and a minimum of 48 hours, turning it each day. I find it far easier to slice if I freeze it for about 4 hours beforehand. Scottish farmed salmon is ideal for this recipe and the price is reasonable. The sweet mustard dill sauce goes well with cured herring too.

PREPARATION TIME: 10 minutes
MARINATING TIME: 48 hours to 5 days

2 lb (900 g) tail piece fresh Scottish salmon

PICKLING INGREDIENTS
4 tablespoons granulated sugar, preferably golden
3 tablespoons coarse sea salt
1 tablespoon sunflower oil
masses of freshly ground black pepper
3 tablespoons chopped fresh dill or 1 good tablespoon dried dill weed

MUSTARD DILL SAUCE
3 tablespoons Dijon mustard
2 tablespoons caster sugar
1 tablespoon white wine vinegar
1 egg yolk
¼ pt (150 ml) sunflower oil
salt
freshly ground black pepper
2 tablespoons chopped fresh dill or 1 tablespoon dried dill weed

Cut the fins off the fish. Lie the tail piece on the board and make a long cut down the back of the salmon slightly above the bone. Slip your fingers over the bone and take off the top fillet, then gently slip the knife under the back bone and pull it out. Pull out any tiny bones that you can see.

Mix the pickling ingredients together in a bowl. Put the two fillets skin side down on the board, spread them with the mixture, then sandwich the fillets together skin side out. Wrap the fish in double foil. Lie it in a dish and place weights on top – a couple of heavy cans will do. Put the dish in the fridge for 48 hours, or up to 5 days, turning every day. (We usually eat the salmon after 2 or 3 days.)

To make the sauce, whisk the mustard, sugar, vinegar and egg yolk together in a bowl (just a little balloon whisk is ideal for this), then incorporate the oil, whisking well. The result will be the consistency of mayonnaise. Season the sauce with salt and pepper and stir in the dill.

To serve the gravad lax, cut it in slices a little thicker than you would for smoked salmon. Cut the slices obliquely to the skin: each slice should then have an edging of dill, which looks so attractive. Serve with the mustard dill sauce.

SERVES 10

Surprisingly Good Salmon Mousse

Canned pink salmon is fine for this mousse, served with brown bread and butter.

PREPARATION TIME: 15 minutes
SETTING TIME: 1 hour

1/2 oz (15 g) powdered gelatine
3 tablespoons cold water
7 1/2 oz (210 g) can pink salmon
1 tablespoon lemon juice
7 fl oz (200 ml) mayonnaise (page 152)
1/4 pint (150 ml) double cream
salt
freshly ground black pepper
sprigs of parsley to garnish

Place the gelatine and water in a small bowl and leave for 3 minutes to form a 'sponge'. Stand the bowl in a pan of simmering water and stir until the gelatine has dissolved, then leave to cool.

Drain the salmon, flake the flesh and remove any pieces of black skin and bone. Place the salmon in a bowl with the lemon juice and mayonnaise and mix thoroughly. Stir in the gelatine.

Whisk the cream until it is thick and just forms soft peaks, then fold it into the salmon mixture with seasoning to taste.

Divide the mixture between five or six small ramekin dishes, smooth the tops and leave in a cool place to set. Garnish each dish with a small sprig of parsley.

SERVES 5 or 6

Avocado Mousse

This mousse looks very pretty when it is turned out, with the avocado peeping out from the mousse mixture. Serve with salad and crusty brown rolls. For more special occasions, fill the centre of the mousse with a prawn mixture. Blend ½ pint (300 ml) mayonnaise with 3 teaspoons tomato purée, the juice of ½ lemon, a little Worcestershire sauce and lots of black pepper. Mix in 12 oz (350 g) well drained shelled prawns.

PREPARATION TIME: 30 minutes
CHILLING TIME: 8 hours

½ oz (15 g) gelatine
3 tablespoons cold water
¼ pint (150 ml) good chicken stock
3 ripe avocado pears
salt
freshly ground black pepper
2 fat cloves garlic, crushed
juice of ½ lemon
½ pint (300 ml) mayonnaise (page 152)
¼ pint (150 ml) double cream, lightly whipped
1 head curly endive, broken into small pieces
a few whole prawns to decorate

Put the gelatine in a bowl with the cold water and leave to stand for about 3 minutes to form a 'sponge', then stand the bowl over a pan of simmering water until dissolved. Allow to cool then stir the gelatine into the stock.

Peel and quarter one of the avocados, removing the stone, and place the flesh in a processor or blender with the stock, salt, pepper, garlic and lemon juice. Reduce to a smooth purée then gently fold in the mayonnaise and cream.

Lightly oil a 2½ pint (1.5 litre) ring mould. Peel the other two avocados, cut them in half and remove the stones. Place the avocados in the ring mould, with their cut surfaces facing upwards. Pour the mousse mixture around them to fill the mould then put it in the fridge to set.

Arrange the endive on a serving plate and turn the mousse out on to this. Decorate with a few whole prawns and serve in slices with more salad.

SERVES 8

Egg Mousse

A great standby. Sometimes I leave out the curry powder and chutney and add chopped watercress or chives to the mixture. If I can get quail's eggs I use them, hard boiled, to decorate the mousse – this makes a most attractive and delicious first course.

PREPARATION AND COOKING TIME: 15 minutes
CHILLING TIME: 1 hour

½ oz (15 g) powdered gelatine
2 tablespoons cold water
10½ oz (298 g) can condensed consommé
¼ pint (150 ml) double cream
6 hard-boiled eggs, chopped
¼ pint (150 ml) mayonnaise (page 152)
1 to 2 teaspoons curry powder
1 tablespoon mango chutney juice
salt
tomato, cucumber and watercress to garnish

Put the gelatine in a small bowl or cup, add the water and leave it to stand for about 3 minutes (the gelatine will form a 'sponge'). Place the bowl in a pan of gently simmering water and stir until the gelatine has dissolved. Put the consommé in a measuring jug and stir in the gelatine.

Whisk the cream until it forms soft peaks. Mix together the cream, eggs, mayonnaise, curry powder and mango chutney juice and stir in three quarters of the consommé. Taste and check seasoning. Divide the mixture between eight individual ramekins and leave to set.

Garnish each ramekin attractively with pieces of tomato, cucumber and watercress, and spoon over the remaining consommé. Chill well before serving.

SERVES 8

Cucumber Mousse

A deliciously light mousse.

PREPARATION TIME: 20 minutes
CHILLING TIME: 8 hours

1 cucumber, peeled, seeded and diced
1 teaspoon salt
½ oz (15 g) powdered gelatine
3 tablespoons water
¼ pint (150 ml) good chicken stock
8 oz (225 g) cream cheese
juice of ½ lemon
¼ pint (150 ml) mayonnaise (page 152)
½ pint (300 ml) whipping cream, whipped
freshly ground black pepper
2 tablespoons snipped chives
1 bunch watercress

Put the cucumber on a plate, sprinkle with salt and leave for about an hour until the juices have run. Rinse the cucumber well under running cold water, then drain thoroughly on kitchen paper.

Put the gelatine in a small bowl, add the water and leave for about 3 minutes to form a 'sponge'. Stand the bowl in a pan of simmering water until the gelatine has dissolved. Allow the gelatine to cool, then stir it into the stock.

Put the cream cheese in a bowl and beat until smooth, then stir in the cucumber and all the remaining ingredients, adding the stock last of all. Taste and check seasoning, then pour into a lightly greased 1½ pint (900 ml) ring mould. Chill the mousse in the refrigerator until set.

When ready to serve, dip the mould into a deep bowl of very hot water for a moment. Put a plate on top of the mould and invert it to turn out the mousse. Fill the centre of the mousse with watercress.

SERVES 8

Brandied Chicken Liver Pâté

A first-rate pâté which is lovely for a dinner party. Make it in advance and keep it in the fridge for a week, or in the freezer for up to a month.

PREPARATION AND COOKING TIME: 1¾ hours
COOLING TIME: 12 hours or overnight

6 rashers streaky bacon, rind removed
1 egg
4 oz (100 g) white bread, crusts removed
4 tablespoons brandy
1 lb (450 g) chicken livers
1 clove garlic, crushed
salt
freshly ground black pepper
scant level teaspoon grated nutmeg
4 oz (100 g) bacon trimmings, cut in small pieces
2 oz (50 g) butter, melted
cucumber and radish slices to garnish

Heat the oven to 325°F/160°C/Gas Mark 3. Stretch the bacon rashers with the back of a knife on a board, then use them to line the base and the sides of a 2 pint (1.2 litre) loaf tin or deep pie dish.

Put the egg into a processor or blender. Break the bread into small pieces and add it to the processor with the brandy and half the chicken livers. Purée and turn the mixture into a bowl. Next put the garlic, remaining chicken livers, seasoning, nutmeg and bacon trimmings in the processor and purée. Add to the first batch of mixture in the bowl. Stir in the melted butter, mix thoroughly and pour into the prepared tin.

Cover the tin with foil and place it in a meat tin containing an inch (2.5 cm) of warm water. Bake in the oven for about 1½ hours. The pâté is cooked if the juices run clear when the centre is pricked with a skewer. Remove the pâté from the oven and leave to become quite cold before turning out on to a serving dish. Garnish with cucumber and radish slices.

SERVES 8

RIGHT: *Lentil Soup (page 14)*

Taramasalata

This smoked cod's roe pâté comes from Greece, and makes a good first course that is a little different. Serve with hot pitta bread, the traditional accompaniment.

PREPARATION TIME: 15 minutes
CHILLING TIME: 1 hour

8 oz (225 g) smoked cod's roe
2 small slices white bread, crusts removed
2 tablespoons milk
1 clove garlic, crushed
4 fl oz (125 ml) olive oil
2 tablespoons lemon juice
salt
freshly ground black pepper

Remove the skin from the cod's roe, place the roe in a processor or blender and purée until smooth.

Soak the bread in the milk, then squeeze out as much milk as possible and add bread to the blender with the garlic. Add the oil to the blender a teaspoonful at a time and purée until all has been absorbed, then blend in the lemon juice and seasoning to taste. Turn the pâté into a small serving dish and chill well before serving.

SERVES 4

LEFT: *Gleneagles Pâté (pages 34–35)*

Gleneagles Pâté

A three-smoked-fish pâté – quite the smartest pâté for a special occasion. Slice when it is very well chilled, and serve with warm granary toast and butter. You will need a processor to make this recipe.

PREPARATION TIME: 1 hour
CHILLING TIME: overnight

4 oz (100 g) smoked salmon slices

TROUT PÂTÉ
6 oz (175 g) smoked trout, skinned
  and boned
3 oz (75 g) butter
3 oz (75 g) cream cheese
juice of 1/2 lemon
salt
freshly ground black pepper

SALMON PÂTÉ
4 oz (100 g) smoked salmon pieces
2 oz (50 g) butter
2 oz (50 g) cream cheese
juice of 1/2 lemon
1 tablespoon tomato purée
salt
freshly ground black pepper

MACKEREL PÂTÉ
6 oz (175 g) smoked mackerel
  fillets, skinned and boned
3 oz (75 g) butter
3 oz (75 g) cream cheese
juice of 1/2 lemon
salt
freshly ground black pepper

Carefully line a 2 pint (1.2 litre) terrine or loaf tin with clingfilm and then line with the slices of smoked salmon.

For the trout pâté, measure all the ingredients into a processor and blend for a few moments until smooth. Turn into the prepared terrine and level out evenly. Stand the terrine in the refrigerator while you prepare the next layer of pâté.

For the salmon pâté, measure all the ingredients into the processor (no need to wash up the bowl in between!) and process until smooth. Carefully spread this mixture in a layer on top of the trout pâté and return the terrine to the refrigerator.

Repeat this process for the mackerel pâté and spread it on top of the salmon pâté. Wrap any surplus clingfilm up and over the top of the pâté and chill in the refrigerator overnight before serving.

SERVES 10

Thomas's Pâté

This is a very good all-purpose pâté, and surprisingly easy to make. Serve with hot toast and butter.

PREPARATION AND COOKING TIME: 1¾ hours
CHILLING TIME: 12 hours or overnight

1 large onion
8 oz (225 g) chicken livers
8 oz (225 g) pork sausagemeat
1 heaped tablespoon chopped parsley
2 cloves garlic, crushed
salt
freshly ground black pepper
about 5 rashers streaky bacon

Heat oven to 325°F/160°C/Gas Mark 3. Peel and quarter the onion and pass it through a mincer with the chicken livers, or put the onion and livers in a blender and purée. Turn into a large bowl with the sausagemeat, parsley, garlic and plenty of seasoning, and mix well together.

Remove the rind and bone from the bacon. Place the rashers on a board and spread each one flat with the back of a knife. Line the bottom and sides of a 1½ pint (900 ml) loaf tin with the bacon, then turn the meat mixture into the tin, spreading the surface flat.

Cover the tin with a piece of foil, place it in a roasting tin half filled with hot water and cook for about 1½ hours. The pâté is cooked if the juices that run out are clear when the centre is pierced with a skewer, and it has slightly shrunk from the sides of the tin.

Cover the pâté with a clean piece of foil weighed down with several weights or heavy cans and leave to become completely cold – better still, chill overnight. Turn the pâté out of the tin and serve in slices.

SERVES 6

Fresh Herb Pâté

If you have lemon thyme in the garden use it instead of common thyme. Add freshly crushed garlic if you like, too. This pâté improves in flavour if you leave it to stand in the refrigerator for a while. Serve with crisp biscuits as a change from toast.

PREPARATION TIME: 5 minutes
CHILLING TIME: 2 hours

6 oz (175 g) cream cheese
¼ pint (150 ml) double cream, lightly whipped
½ level teaspoon freshly chopped thyme
½ teaspoon freshly chopped dill
1 teaspoon freshly chopped chives
salt
freshly ground black pepper

Blend together the cheese and cream and stir in the herbs and seasoning. Turn into a ¾ pint (450 ml) dish, cover and chill well before serving.

SERVES 4

Crudités

Crudités are pieces of raw vegetables served with a thick mayonnaise-type sauce as a dip, either as a first course or with drinks. For a really simple curry dip, add ½ to 1 teaspoon curry powder, ½ teaspoon French mustard, 1 table-spoon mango chutney juice and 1 teaspoon lemon juice to ½ pint (300 ml) mayonnaise, and mix well. If you are having a dinner party, it is nice to make two or three dips and put them in the centre of the table with a selection of vegetables and let people help themselves.

PREPARATION TIME: 20 minutes

4 oz (100 g) mange-tout
1 small head of fennel
2 carrots, peeled
2 to 3 sticks celery
1 onion
½ cucumber
1 small cauliflower
1 red pepper
1 green pepper
1 bunch radishes

Top and tail the mange-tout and slice the fennel lengthways. Cut the carrots and celery into strips about 2 inches (5 cm) long and ¼ inch (6 mm) square. Cut the onion into thin rings. Leave the peel on the cucumber and cut it into wedges. Break the cauliflower into tiny sprigs, leaving a small piece of stalk on each so that they are easy to pick up. Cut the peppers into strips, removing all white pith and seeds. Wash the radishes and cut off the roots, leaving on about ¼ inch (6 mm) of the green stalk. Make four slicing cuts down into each radish from the root end, and then leave in a bowl of iced water to open like flowers.

Take a large flat dish and place a bowl of dip in the centre. Arrange the vegetables in neat piles around it.

SERVES 4 to 6

Avocado Dip

This creamy dip makes an interesting first course when there are just four people around a small table and everyone can easily stretch to the centre bowl. Serve with crudités (*opposite page*).

PREPARATION TIME: 10 minutes

2 ripe avocado pears
5 tablespoons double cream
2 oz (50 g) cream cheese
½ level teaspoon dry mustard
2 level teaspoons caster sugar
2 tablespoons lemon juice
salt
freshly ground black pepper
small sprig of watercress to garnish

Cut the avocados in half and remove the stones. Scoop the flesh into a bowl and mash with a fork until smooth.

Blend together the cream and cream cheese, then stir into the avocado purée until well mixed. Season with the mustard, sugar, lemon juice and plenty of salt and pepper. Pile the mixture into a small serving dish and garnish with the watercress.

SERVES 4

FISH COURSES

Now that so many people are showing an interest in fish, the best super-markets sell a wide variety of top-quality fish. Try not to make up your mind what to buy until you have seen what your fishmonger has to offer – then choose whatever looks good.

Some of the less expensive fish, such as coley and whiting, can be excellent. Don't be put off if some of them aren't as pretty to look at as the more costly varieties!

Extraordinarily Good Double Fish Pie

Mixing smoked and unsmoked fish adds interest to the pie. Do use a shallow dish so that everyone gets plenty of the crispy brown topping.

PREPARATION AND COOKING TIME: 55 minutes

12 oz (350 g) smoked haddock
12 oz (350 g) unsmoked haddock
1 pint (600 ml) milk
2 oz (50 g) butter
2 oz (50 g) flour
6 oz (175 g) button mushrooms,
*   sliced*
½ teaspoon grated nutmeg
juice of ½ lemon
salt
freshly ground black pepper

POTATO TOPPING
1 lb (450 g) potatoes
milk and butter for mashing
4 oz (100 g) mature Cheddar
*   cheese, grated*
salt
freshly ground black pepper

Boil the potatoes for the topping until they are tender. Meanwhile, put the fish in a pan with the milk and simmer gently for 10 minutes or until the fish can be flaked with a fork. Strain and reserve the milk. Skin and flake the fish, removing any bones.

Rinse out the pan. Melt the butter, add the flour and cook for a minute, then gradually blend in the reserved milk and bring to the boil, stirring until thickened. Add the mushrooms and simmer for about 2 minutes. Add the nutmeg, lemon juice and flaked fish, mix well, then taste and check seasoning. Turn into a shallow 3 pint (1.75 litre) greased ovenproof dish.

Drain the potatoes and mash with plenty of milk and butter, then stir in three quarters of the cheese and seasoning. (The mixture should be fairly soft, like whipped cream.) Transfer the potato to a piping bag fitted with a nozzle, and pipe zig-zags over the fish from side to side of the dish. Sprinkle the remaining cheese over the potato.

Cook in the oven at 425°F/220°C/Gas Mark 7 for 30 to 40 minutes, until the topping is golden brown. Serve at once.

SERVES 6

Mediterranean Fish Casserole

Serve with lots of crisp garlic bread.

PREPARATION AND COOKING TIME: 30 minutes

1½ lb (675 g) monkfish, skinned
1½ oz (40 g) butter
1 large onion, chopped
1 clove garlic, crushed
14 oz (397 g) can chopped tomatoes
¼ pint (150 ml) dry vermouth
2 sprigs of lemon thyme
salt
freshly ground black pepper
2 oz (50 g) peeled prawns, drained
freshly chopped parsley

Cut the fish into 1 inch (2.5 cm) cubes. Melt the butter in a large shallow pan, add the onion and fry until almost tender and pale golden brown. Add the garlic, tomatoes, vermouth, thyme and seasoning. Boil the sauce rapidly for 5 minutes to reduce it slightly. Taste to check seasoning then add the fish and cook for a further 5 minutes, or until the fish is firm and white.

Remove the thyme, turn into a warm serving dish and serve scattered with prawns and freshly chopped parsley.

SERVES 6

Sole Florentine

No need to cook the fish before the dish is assembled.

PREPARATION AND COOKING TIME: 1 hour

4 large sole fillets, skinned
salt
freshly ground black pepper
juice of ½ small lemon
1½ oz (40 g) butter
1½ oz (40 g) flour
¾ pint (450 ml) milk
1 lb (450 g) frozen cut-leaf spinach, thawed and drained
3 oz (75 g) well-flavoured Cheddar cheese, grated
¾ oz (20 g) fresh white breadcrumbs

Heat the oven to 400°F/200°C/Gas Mark 6. Season the fillets well with salt, pepper and lemon juice, roll them up and set to one side.

Melt the butter in a pan, add the flour and cook for a minute. Gradually blend in the milk and bring to the boil, stirring until thickened. Simmer for 2 minutes and season to taste.

Blend half of the sauce with the spinach and spread in a shallow 3 pint (1.75 litre) ovenproof dish. Arrange the fish on top and pour over the remaining sauce. Mix the cheese and breadcrumbs together and sprinkle on top of the sauce. Bake in the oven for 30 to 40 minutes until the topping is pale brown and the fish perfectly white all through.

SERVES 4

Stuffed Plaice

Use any flat fish that looks a good buy when you are at the fishmongers. Test the fish near the bone to make sure that it is cooked through.

PREPARATION AND COOKING TIME: 1 hour

4 oz (100 g) fresh brown breadcrumbs
4 tablespoons freshly chopped parsley
a little fresh thyme
6 spring onions, finely chopped
grated rind and juice of 1 lemon
salt
freshly ground black pepper
2 eggs
4 whole plaice, about 12 oz (350 g) each
a little butter
2 tomatoes, sliced

To make the stuffing, put the breadcrumbs in a bowl with the parsley, thyme, spring onions, lemon rind and juice and seasoning. Lightly beat the eggs and stir into the breadcrumbs, mixing all well together.

Clean and remove the heads from the fish, and trim the fins and tails with scissors. Place each fish, dark-skinned side down, on a board and with a sharp knife make a cut through the white skin along the backbone to within ¾ inch (1.5 cm) of the head and tail. Ease the flesh away from either side of the bone to form two large pockets. Fill the pockets with stuffing.

Lightly butter a shallow ovenproof dish, and lay the fish in it. Dot with a little more butter, cover with foil and cook in the oven at 400°F/200°C/Gas Mark 6 for about 20 minutes, until the fish is just tender. Arrange the tomato slices on top of the stuffing and return the fish to the oven for a further 10 minutes. To serve, lift the fish on to warmed individual serving plates.

SERVES 4

Cod Provençale

To vary this simple dish, add 6 oz (175 g) peeled prawns to the sauce with the seasoning and parsley. Serve with a crisp green vegetable, such as broccoli.

PREPARATION AND COOKING TIME: 35 minutes

1 oz (25 g) butter
1 medium onion, chopped
4 oz (100 g) button mushrooms, sliced
14 oz (397 g) can chopped tomatoes
1 teaspoon light muscovado sugar
salt
freshly ground black pepper
2 tablespoons freshly chopped parsley
1 lb (450 g) fillet of cod, divided into four equal pieces

Heat the oven to 375°F/180°C/Gas Mark 5. Melt the butter in a saucepan and quickly fry the onion for about 5 minutes, until soft. Add the mushrooms and tomatoes, bring to the boil, and simmer until thick and pulpy. Stir in the sugar, seasoning to taste and half the parsley. Turn the sauce into a 2 pint (1.2 litre) ovenproof dish.

Arrange the pieces of cod on top of the sauce then bake in the oven for about 25 minutes, until the fish is cooked (it should be white all through).

Serve sprinkled with the remaining chopped parsley.

SERVES 4

Haddock Kedgeree

Look for smoked haddock that has not been artificially coloured.

PREPARATION AND COOKING TIME: 30 minutes

6 oz (150 g) long-grain rice
2 hard-boiled eggs
12 oz (350 g) smoked haddock fillets
2 oz (50 g) butter
juice of 1/2 lemon
salt
cayenne pepper
sprigs of parsley to garnish

Cook the rice in plenty of boiling salted water, as directed on the packet. Rinse well, drain and keep warm. Cut a few slices of egg and reserve for garnish, then roughly chop the remainder.

Poach the haddock in a little water for about 10 minutes. Drain and remove all skin and any bones, then flake the flesh.

Melt the butter in a large pan, add the rice, eggs and fish, and heat through slowly. Stir in the lemon juice, and add salt and cayenne pepper to taste. Pile the kedgeree into a warmed dish and serve garnished with sprigs of parsley and slices of egg.

SERVES 4

Pan-Fried Mackerel

If the mackerel have not been cleaned, slit them along the belly with a sharp knife and remove the gut; wash thoroughly and remove the eyes.

PREPARATION AND COOKING TIME: 15 minutes

4 mackerel, cleaned
seasoned flour
1 oz (25 g) butter
1 tablespoon sunflower oil
2 tablespoons Sesame Seed Crunch (page 154)
lemon wedges and fresh parsley to garnish

Wash the mackerel under running cold water to remove any loose blood, and coat in seasoned flour.

Melt the butter and oil in a large frying pan and fry the fish for about 8 minutes, turning once. Remove from the pan and arrange on a warm serving dish. Sprinkle with Sesame Seed Crunch and serve garnished with lemon wedges and parsley.

SERVES 4

Quenelles
with Spinach and Sorrel Sauce

To prepare the quenelles ahead, poach as suggested in the recipe, arrange in an ovenproof dish, cover with foil and keep in the refrigerator until required. Reheat in the oven at 300°F/150°C/Gas Mark 2 for about 40 minutes, adding the sauce just before serving. Warm brioches (*page 227*) are a delicious accompaniment.

PREPARATION AND COOKING TIME: 30 minutes
CHILLING TIME: 6 hours

1 lb (450 g) cod fillets, skinned and boned
12 oz (350 g) smoked mackerel fillets, skinned
3 egg whites
salt
freshly ground black pepper
1/4 teaspoon ground mace
8 fl oz (225 ml) double cream

SAUCE
1/4 pint (150 ml) white wine
1 oz (25 g) fresh spinach
6 leaves fresh sorrel
salt
freshly ground black pepper
juice of 1/2 lemon

Roughly chop the fish and place in a processor with the egg whites, salt, pepper and mace. Process for a few moments until absolutely smooth then, with the processor running, add the cream in a steady stream until thoroughly blended. Take care not to over-process, otherwise the cream may turn to butter. Turn the mixture into a bowl, cover with clingfilm and chill in the refrigerator for several hours before cooking.

Meanwhile, make the spinach and sorrel purée for the sauce. Pour the wine into a saucepan and boil rapidly until reduced to a thin syrup, then remove the pan from the heat. Blanch the spinach and sorrel in a pan of boiling salted water for a minute, then refresh under running cold water. Drain well. Put the spinach and sorrel in the processor with the wine syrup and reduce to a smooth purée. Turn into a bowl, cover with clingfilm and refrigerate until needed.

Pour the double cream into a saucepan, bring to the boil and cook until it will coat the back of a metal spoon. Stir in the spinach and sorrel purée and add seasoning and lemon juice to taste. Pour the sauce over the quenelles and serve sprinkled with chopped parsley.

SERVES 6

Pink Trout with Dill

Farmed trout is now available in most parts of Britain. Prepare and cook the fish the day before it is needed, and serve with Cucumber and Dill Mayonnaise (*opposite page*) – ½ pint (300 ml) will be sufficient to serve six.

PREPARATION AND COOKING TIME: 1 hour
CHILLING TIME: overnight

6 pink-fleshed trout, about 10 oz (275 g) each, cleaned
juice of 1 lemon
12 black peppercorns
a little salt
slices of cucumber and fresh dill to decorate

Heat the oven to 400°F/200°/Gas Mark 6. Arrange the cleaned fish in a large roasting tin, and add the lemon juice, peppercorns and salt. Cover with boiling water and a lid of foil, then poach in the oven for 30 to 40 minutes, until the flesh has become matt pink (test along the backbone). Remove the fish from the oven and leave covered until lukewarm, then drain off the water.

Skin the fish and discard the heads. Lift the top fillet gently off the bone, pull out the bone and then carefully replace the fillet. Arrange the six fish on a flat tray that will go in the fridge, cover with clingfilm and chill overnight.

To serve, arrange cucumber slices down the centre of each fish and decorate with dill.

SERVES 6

Fresh Scotch Salmon

There is really nothing more special than salmon for a buffet. Scottish farmed salmon are usually a good buy all the year round, coming from the lochs of the West of Scotland where they are bred. Always remember that, like all fish, salmon needs very little cooking. Another good sauce to serve with salmon can be made by mixing ½ pint (300 ml) mayonnaise with ½ pint (300 ml) soured cream and the juice of 1 lemon.

PREPARATION AND COOKING TIME: 30 minutes
CHILLING TIME: overnight

6 lb (2.75 kg) fresh salmon
1 onion, peeled and quartered
12 black peppercorns
2 bay leaves
4 tablespoons white wine vinegar
cucumber slices and fresh dill or
    parsley to decorate

**CUCUMBER AND DILL
MAYONNAISE**
½ cucumber
1 pint (600 ml) mayonnaise (page
    152)
2 tablespoons chopped fresh dill

Lift the salmon into a fish kettle, and add the onion, peppercorns, bay leaves and vinegar with just enough water to cover. Put the lid on, bring slowly to the boil, then simmer gently for 12 minutes. Remove from the heat and leave until the fish is warm but not hot, which will take about 4 hours.

To cook the salmon in an oven, if you don't have a fish kettle, remove the head, season the fish well, and wrap in buttered foil. Lift into a large meat tin, and pour in sufficient boiling water to come halfway up the fish. Cook at 400°F/200°C/Gas Mark 6 for 1 hour, turning the fish once during cooking. Leave the fish to become lukewarm.

Drain the fish, lift out on to a work surface, and carefully peel off the skin. Lay the fish on a serving platter, cover with clingfilm and chill overnight or until required.

Just before serving, peel and seed the cucumber, cut it into small dice, and stir into the mayonnaise with the dill. Decorate the salmon with the cucumber slices and fresh dill or parsley.

SERVES 12

Salmon en Croûte

A stunning centrepiece for a dinner party that can be prepared a day ahead, chilled in the fridge, then baked an hour before it is needed. The sauce, too, can be made ahead and reheated when required.

PREPARATION AND COOKING TIME: 1¼ hours

3 lb (1.4 kg) tail piece of fresh salmon	**FRESH HERB SAUCE**
juice of ½ lemon	3 oz (75 g) butter
salt	juice of 1 lemon
freshly ground black pepper	1 rounded teaspoon flour
2 oz (50 g) butter	½ pint (300 ml) single cream
1 tablespoon freshly snipped chives	1 egg yolk
12 oz (350 g) packet frozen puff pastry, thawed	salt
1 egg, beaten	freshly ground black pepper
	1 tablespoon freshly snipped chives or dill

First bone the salmon. Slide the knife on top of the backbone and take off the first fillet. Turn the fish over and do the same on the other side, to take off the second fillet. To remove the skin, lay each fillet, skin side down, on a chopping board. With a sharp knife and using a sawing action, work along the fillet from the tail, pressing the knife down on to the fish skin at an angle until the skin is removed. Pull out any bones from the fillets.

Squeeze the lemon juice over the fish and season well. Spread half the butter over one fillet, then sprinkle with chives. Put the other fillet on top the opposite way round and spread with the remaining butter. Roll out the pastry thinly and use it to wrap the fish, sealing the pastry very thoroughly with beaten egg. Bake in the oven at 425°F/220°C/Gas Mark 7 for 35 to 40 minutes, until golden brown.

To make the sauce, put all the ingredients except the herbs in a processor or blender and blend until smooth. Transfer to a bowl, stand the bowl over a pan of simmering water and stir until thick. Season to taste then add the herbs.

When the salmon is cooked, serve straight away with the warm sauce.

SERVES 8

Simply Grilled Fresh Fish

Grilling fish is both quick and inexpensive and is suitable for small whole fish such as mackerel, herrings and sardines. The fish should be washed and cleaned and then scored with three diagonal cuts on each side of the body. Season and spread with a little soft butter and grill under a moderate grill, basting and turning once during cooking. Allow about 10 to 15 minutes for the entire cooking time for whole fish, depending on the size and thickness. When the fish is cooked the flesh flakes easily when tested with a knife and will lift off the bone.

Grilling may also be used for cutlets, steaks and fillets of flat fish or cod or haddock. There is no need to slash the flesh, just season and spread with melted or soft butter. Fillets of plaice or sole will only need about 4 to 5 minutes cooking time and no turning. Cod and haddock fillets will need 8 to 10 minutes depending on the thickness, while cutlets and steaks will need about the same time as a whole fish and should be turned once.

Quick Tartare Sauce

Stir 1 tablespoon each chopped gherkins, chopped capers and chopped parsley into ¼ pint (150 ml) mayonnaise (*page 152*).

Serve this sauce with any plain fried or grilled fish. Spare sauce may be stored in a screw-topped jar in the refrigerator.

As a variation, replace half the mayonnaise with soured cream or yoghurt. Store the sauce in the refrigerator and use within 3 or 4 days.

Prawn Creole

This dish is a meal in itself, but if you like you could serve it with a crisp green salad, lightly tossed in French dressing (*page 153*). Use whatever small pasta shapes you have in store.

PREPARATION AND COOKING TIME: 30 minutes

1 medium-sized onion, finely chopped
2 tablespoons oil
3 sticks celery, sliced
1 green pepper, seeded and cut in strips
1 clove garlic, crushed
14 oz (397 g) can chopped tomatoes
½ pint (300 ml) dry cider
1 tablespoon tomato purée
salt
freshly ground black pepper
4 oz (100 g) penne
8 oz (225 g) peeled prawns

Fry the onion in the oil for about 2 minutes, then stir in the celery, green pepper and garlic and fry for a further 5 minutes. Stir in the tomatoes, cider, tomato purée and seasoning and bring to the boil. Add the penne, stir to mix thoroughly, then cover the saucepan with a lid and simmer gently for about 15 minutes.

Remove the lid from the saucepan, stir in the prawns and simmer gently for 5 minutes. Taste and check seasoning, then turn into a warm serving dish.

SERVES 4

Moules Marinière

Make sure that every mussel is tightly closed before they are cooked. This means that they are all alive and there are no bad ones. This dish could also be made with fresh cockles: the tightly closed shells should be left in a bucket of lightly salted water for an hour, then scrubbed before proceeding.

PREPARATION AND COOKING TIME: 30 minutes

4 pints (2.3 litres) fresh mussels
2 oz (50 g) butter
1 onion, finely chopped
4 stalks parsley
2 sprigs fresh thyme
1 bay leaf
freshly ground black pepper
½ pint (300 ml) white wine
salt
½ oz (15 g) flour
freshly chopped parsley

Scrape and clean each mussel with a strong knife to remove all seaweed, mud and beard. Wash thoroughly in several changes of water, then drain.

Melt 1 oz (25 g) of the butter in a large saucepan over a low heat, add the onion and fry until soft but not coloured. Add the herbs, pepper, wine, salt and mussels, cover the saucepan with a tightly fitting lid and cook quickly, shaking the pan constantly, until the mussels open (about 5 to 6 minutes). Lift the mussels out, discarding the empty half shells, and keep warm in a covered dish.

Cream the remaining butter with the flour. Remove the herbs from the cooking liquor, then drop the creamed butter and flour into the stock a teaspoonful at a time and whisk until the sauce has thickened. Taste and check seasoning. Pour the sauce over the mussels and serve sprinkled with chopped parsley.

SERVES 4

MEAT DISHES

Where meat is concerned, we now have more choice than ever before. Cuts are leaner, so even though meat may seem expensive you are not paying for a lot of unwanted fat. If you use good-quality non-stick pans, you need not add much fat when you cook either. Do consider grilling rather than frying things such as bacon and steaks.

When buying a joint for a special occasion, try to remember to buy it ahead of time so that it can mature in the refrigerator for a few days. If you buy your weekend meat on, say, Wednesday, there is likely to be more choice too.

Boiled Beef and Carrots

Remember to warn the butcher to brine the meat for you. Ideally, let him know 10 days beforehand. It is essential to simmer the joint slowly otherwise it will shrink.

PREPARATION AND COOKING TIME: 2½ hours

3½ lb (1.5 kg) boned and rolled salt silverside
1 lb (450 g) small whole onions
1 lb (450 g) small whole carrots
8 sticks celery, sliced
8 medium potatoes, halved
2 tablespoons chopped parsley

MUSTARD SAUCE
2 oz (50 g) butter
2 oz (50 g) flour
½ pint (300 ml) milk
½ pint (300 ml) stock from the beef
1 level tablespoon dry mustard
1 level tablespoon sugar
3 tablespoons vinegar
salt
freshly ground black pepper

Wash the meat in cold water and, if necessary, soak overnight to remove any excess salt. Place the meat in a large saucepan in plenty of water and cover with a lid or foil. Bring to the boil, then simmer very gently for 2 hours, checking to make sure there is still enough water. Add the vegetables and continue cooking for a further hour.

Lift the meat on to a serving dish. Remove the vegetables with a slotted spoon and spoon them around the meat. Keep warm, and when ready to serve sprinkle the vegetables with parsley.

To make the sauce, melt the butter in a saucepan, add the flour and cook, stirring, for 2 minutes. Stir in the milk and stock from the beef and bring to the boil, stirring constantly. Simmer for 2 minutes to thicken. Blend together the mustard, sugar and vinegar and stir into the sauce. Cook for one minute, then add salt and pepper. Serve with the meat.

Serves 8 to 10

Highgate Beef with Prunes

An ideal recipe for a crowd, or to make for freezing.

PREPARATION AND COOKING TIME: 2 hours

8 oz (225 g) prunes, soaked overnight and stoned
a little sunflower oil
3 lb (1.5 kg) chuck steak, cubed
2 oz (50 g) flour
2 tablespoons soy sauce
3 tablespoons clear honey
4 tablespoons vinegar
¾ pint (450 ml) water
salt
freshly ground black pepper
8 oz (225 g) button mushrooms

Heat the oven to 325°F/160°C/Gas Mark 3. Brown the meat, in batches, in a little oil in a non-stick pan, then transfer to a fireproof casserole with a slotted spoon, draining well. Sprinkle the flour over the meat and stir over the heat, adding the soy sauce, honey, vinegar, water and seasoning. Bring to the boil, stirring until thickened, then cover and simmer for 5 minutes.

Transfer the casserole to the oven and cook for about an hour. Remove from the oven, stir in the mushrooms and drained prunes, and bring to the boil again. Leave to simmer for 5 minutes, then return to the oven for a further 30 minutes, or until the meat is tender. Taste and check seasoning before serving.

SERVES 8 to 10

Beef in Horseradish Cream

The flavour of the sauce is really different. It can all be prepared well in advance, with the horseradish cream stirred in at the last minute.

PREPARATION AND COOKING TIME: 2½ hours

2 lb (900 g) stewing steak
8 oz (225 g) onions, chopped
1 teaspoon curry powder
1 teaspoon ground ginger
1 teaspoon muscovado sugar
1½ oz (40 g) flour
¾ pint (450 ml) good beef stock
2 tablespoons Worcestershire sauce
salt
freshly ground black pepper
3 heaped tablespoons horseradish cream
a little freshly chopped parsley

Heat the oven to 325°F/160°C/Gas Mark 3. Cut the meat into neat 1 inch (2.5 cm) cubes. Turn into a large fireproof casserole and heat gently until the fat begins to run freely from the meat. Increase the heat and fry until the meat has browned on all sides. Add the onion, curry powder, ginger, sugar and flour and cook for a minute. Stir in the stock, Worcestershire sauce and seasoning, cover with a lid and transfer to the oven for about 2 hours, or until the meat is tender.

When ready to serve, stir in the horseradish cream. Sprinkle with chopped parsley and serve at once.

SERVES 6

Highland Beef
with Herbed Dumplings

A lovely dish for a cold day.

PREPARATION AND COOKING TIME: 2½ hours

1 lb (450 g) stewing steak, cubed
1 oz (25 g) seasoned flour
2 tablespoons sunflower oil
1 large onion, sliced
¾ pint (450 ml) good beef stock
2 good tablespoons tomato purée
¼ teaspoon mixed dried herbs
salt
freshly ground black pepper

DUMPLINGS
4 oz (100 g) self-raising flour
salt
freshly ground black pepper
2 oz (50 g) shredded suet
2 tablespoons freshly chopped parsley
about 4 tablespoons cold water

Heat the oven to 325°F/160°C/Gas Mark 3. Toss the meat in the seasoned flour. Heat the oil in a large pan, add the onion and cook for about 5 minutes until golden brown. Add the meat and any remaining seasoned flour and fry quickly until browned all over, then gradually blend in stock, tomato purée and herbs. Bring to the boil, stirring all the time, then turn into a 2 pint (1.2 litre) casserole dish. Season, cover with a lid and cook in the oven for about 2 hours, until the meat is tender.

Mix all the ingredients for the dumplings and shape into eight small balls. The mixture should be a soft dough and not too sticky to handle. Add the dumplings to the casserole for the last 25 to 35 minutes of cooking time.

SERVES 4

Salcombe Beef

Most of our family summer holidays have been at Salcombe. I remember on many occasions leaving this in the oven to cook itself while we were on the beach – a great welcome to come home to.

PREPARATION AND COOKING TIME: 3 hours

2 oz (50 g) flour
freshly ground black pepper
1½ lb (675 g) chuck steak, cubed
2 tablespoons sunflower oil
2 medium-sized onions, chopped
8 oz (225 g) carrots, peeled and sliced
6 sticks celery, chopped
1 pint (600 ml) good beef stock
1 sprig parsley
1 sprig thyme
2 bay leaves
1 small orange, quartered and pips removed
1 level tablespoon redcurrant jelly
8 oz (225 g) mushrooms, sliced

Heat the oven to 325°F/160°C/Gas Mark 3. Put the flour, salt and pepper in a polythene bag then add the meat and shake well so that the meat is evenly coated. Melt the oil in a large pan and fry the meat for about 10 minutes until browned all over. Lift out on to a plate with a slotted spoon.

Add the onions, carrots and celery to the fat left in the pan and fry for about 5 minutes until just beginning to soften, then add any flour left from coating the meat. Gradually stir in the stock, then add the meat, herbs, orange and redcurrant jelly and transfer to a fireproof casserole. Bring to the boil, cover and transfer to the oven for 2 hours, then add the mushrooms and cook for about another 30 minutes, until the meat is tender. Remove the orange quarters and herbs before serving.

SERVES 4 to 6

Cold Roast Fillet of Beef

And now for a little sheer luxury – very expensive, but there's no waste. Occasionally there is a reason to have such a family celebration lunch in summer. A whole fillet weighs about 3½ to 4½ lb (1.5 to 2 kg) and you will get about four servings to the pound (450 g). You need a good-sized piece for the best results. Ask the butcher to tie it with string and prepare it for you. Cook it the day before, then chill it before slicing.

To roast, first rub a little butter all over the fillet and season with salt and freshly ground black pepper. Roast at 425°F/220°C/Gas Mark 7 for 12 minutes to the pound (450 g). This will give a brown outside and a pink centre. Leave the meat to cool, then chill overnight.

Slice just before serving (not more than 2 hours ahead), and arrange attractively on a large flat dish. Garnish with small sprigs of parsley and watercress and serve with mustard and Fresh Horseradish Sauce.

Fresh Horseradish Sauce

Lightly whip ¼ pint (150 ml) double cream and add 2 level tablespoons freshly grated horseradish (homegrown is best). Stir in a teaspoon of cider or wine vinegar, some salt and pepper and a little caster sugar, and blend thoroughly. Turn into a small serving dish, cover with clingfilm or foil and chill well before serving with hot or cold roast beef and steaks.

This quantity of sauce will be enough for eight, so make about twice as much if you are serving a whole fillet.

St. James Beef

Plenty of rich spicy sauce with this casserole so serve with creamy mashed potato or rice.

PREPARATION AND COOKING TIME: 2½ hours

2 lb (900 g) lean stewing beef
3 tablespoons sunflower oil
1½ oz (40 g) flour
¾ pt (450 ml) good beef stock
2 tablespoons Worcestershire sauce
2 tablespoons redcurrant jelly
4 oz (100 g) button mushrooms, quartered
a little salt
freshly ground black pepper

Heat the oven to 325°F/160°C/Gas Mark 3. Cut the meat into ¾ inch (2 cm) cubes. Measure the oil into a large non-stick pan and brown meat on all sides. Sprinkle in the flour, turning the meat at the same time, then stir in the stock. Add the Worcestershire sauce, redcurrant jelly and mushrooms. Season lightly, bring to the boil and simmer for 5 minutes.

Transfer to an ovenproof casserole and cook in the oven for about 2 hours, until the meat is tender. Taste and check seasoning before serving.

SERVES 6

Pepper Pot Beef

The kidney beans stretch the meat and this is a good dish for an inexpensive buffet supper.

PREPARATION AND COOKING TIME: 3 hours

1 oz (25 g) flour
salt
freshly ground black pepper
1 level teaspoon ground ginger
2 lb (900 g) chuck steak, cubed
3 tablespoons sunflower oil

SAUCE
¼ teaspoon Tabasco sauce
8 oz (225 g) can chopped tomatoes
2 level tablespoons light muscovado sugar
2 tablespoons white wine vinegar
2 cloves garlic, crushed
1 bay leaf
1 red pepper, seeded and sliced
15 oz (425 g) can red kidney beans, drained
4 oz (100 g) button mushrooms, sliced

Heat the oven to 325°F/160°C/Gas Mark 3. Put the flour, salt, pepper and ginger into a polythene bag, add the meat and shake well until the meat is coated with the flour. Heat the oil in a large pan, add the meat and fry quickly until browned all over. Lift out and put into a 3 pint (1.7 litre) casserole dish.

In a bowl, mix all the ingredients for the sauce except the red pepper, kidney beans and mushrooms, then pour over the meat. Cover the casserole with a lid or a piece of foil and cook in the oven for about 2 hours. Add the red pepper, beans and mushrooms and return to the oven for a further 30 minutes, or until the meat is tender. Remove the bay leaf, taste and check seasoning.

SERVES 6

RIGHT: *Sole Florentine (page 43)*
OVERLEAF LEFT: *Quenelles with Spinach and Sorrel Sauce (pages 48–49) and Brioches (page 227)*
OVERLEAF RIGHT: *Steak and Kidney Pie (page 67)*

Slow-Roast Brisket

A good lean piece of brisket slow-roasts beautifully – ask your butcher to prepare it for you by removing all the excess fat and bone. Don't expect the middle to be pink but do expect it to be tender. It makes an economical Sunday lunch with roast potatoes and Yorkshire pudding. Make a gravy from the stock and meat juices.

PREPARATION AND COOKING TIME: 3½ hours

3 lb (1.5 kg) lean brisket, boned and rolled
1 beef stock cube
about ½ pint (300 ml) water
salt
freshly ground black pepper

Heat the oven to 425°F/220°C/Gas Mark 7. Put the meat in a small meat tin, and add the stock cube and sufficient water to give a depth of 1 inch (2.5 cm). Season with salt and pepper. Cover the tin with a lid or piece of foil and cook in the oven for 30 minutes. Lower the heat to 300°F/150°C/Gas Mark 2 for 50 minutes per pound (450 g) of meat. Turn the heat up to 400°F/200°C/Gas Mark 6 for the last 45 minutes of the cooking time to allow roast potatoes to brown and a Yorkshire pudding to cook.

SERVES 6

LEFT: *Moussaka (page 79)*

Old English Oxtail

If you use a non-stick frying pan there is no need for any extra fat as the oxtail has plenty of its own, even when trimmed.

PREPARATION AND COOKING TIME: 4½ to 5½ hours

3 lb (1.5 kg) oxtail, in pieces
2 rashers streaky bacon, cut into strips
2 onions, sliced
3 carrots, sliced
8 sticks celery, chopped
2 oz (50 g) flour
1½ pints (900 ml) good beef stock
2 bay leaves
3 sprigs parsley
salt
freshly ground black pepper

Heat the oven to 325°F/160°C/Gas Mark 3.

Trim off any excess fat from the oxtail joints. Brown really well on all sides in a non-stick pan, then transfer to a fireproof casserole. Fry the bacon strips in the pan for about 5 minutes, then add the chopped vegetables and cook for a further 4 to 5 minutes. Add the flour and stock, stir well and cook until beginning to thicken. Pour over the meat and add remaining ingredients. Bring to the boil, cover and simmer for 5 minutes.

Transfer the casserole to the oven and cook for 4 to 5 hours, or until tender. Take care to skim off any excess fat once the oxtail is cooked (this is much more easily done if the dish is allowed to get cold and the fat sets). Taste and check seasoning before serving.

SERVES 6

Steak and Kidney Pie

The pastry for this pie is my mother's recipe. It is essential to use a hard margarine straight from the refrigerator. I use this same pastry for fruit pies, too.

PREPARATION AND COOKING TIME: 2¾ hours
COOLING TIME: 2 hours

1 lb (450 g) skirt beef
4 oz (100 g) ox kidney
1 oz (25 g) flour
2 tablespoons oil
1 large onion, chopped
½ pint (300 ml) good beef stock
salt
freshly ground black pepper
4 oz (100 g) mushrooms, sliced

FLAKY PASTRY
8 oz (225 g) strong plain flour
½ teaspoon salt
6 oz (175 g) hard margarine
scant ¼ pint (150 ml) cold water
a little beaten egg to glaze

Cut the steak and kidney into 1 inch (2.5 cm) pieces, put in a polythene bag with the flour and toss until well coated. Heat the oil in a saucepan, add the meat and fry with the onion until browned. Stir in the stock and seasoning and bring to the boil. Partially cover the pan and simmer for about 1½ hours, then stir in the mushrooms and continue cooking for a further 30 minutes or until the meat is tender. Taste and check seasoning, turn into a 1½ pint (900 ml) pie dish and allow to become cold. Put a pie funnel in the centre.

To make the pastry, sift the flour and salt into a mixing bowl. Coarsely grate the margarine into the bowl. Stir in just sufficient water to make a firm dough and then roll out on a lightly floured surface to make a strip about ½ inch (1.25 cm) thick and 6 inches (15 cm) wide. Fold the pastry in three and give it a quarter turn to the left. Roll out again into a strip and fold in three. Wrap the pastry in foil and chill in the fridge for 30 minutes.

Heat the oven to 425°F/220°C/Gas Mark 7. Roll out the pastry on a lightly floured table and use to cover the pie. Seal and crimp the edges and use any pastry trimming to decorate the top with pastry leaves. Brush the pie with a little beaten egg and make a small hole in the centre for the steam to escape. Bake in the oven for about 40 minutes, until the pastry is golden brown and the meat is hot all through (if the pastry is browning too much, reduce the heat to 350°F/180°C/Gas Mark 4).

SERVES 4 to 6

Steak and Kidney Pudding

Very traditional and so popular on a chilly day when everyone is starving. Make extra gravy if your family are gravy addicts like mine!

PREPARATION AND COOKING TIME: 4½ hours

1½ lb (675 g) skirt beef
8 oz (225 g) ox kidney
1 rounded tablespoon flour
1 small onion, finely chopped
4 oz (100 g) mushrooms, sliced
salt
freshly ground black pepper
about ¼ pint (150 ml) good beef
*   stock*

SUET PASTRY
8 oz (225 g) self-raising flour
salt
3 oz (75 g) shredded suet
8 tablespoons (120 ml) cold water

Grease a 1½ or 2 pint (about 1 litre) pudding basin. Cut the steak and kidney into ½ inch (1.25 cm) cubes, discarding any fat and the core from the kidney. Toss in the flour with the onion, mushrooms and seasoning.

Next, prepare the pastry. Put the flour, salt and suet in a bowl and mix with the water to a soft but not sticky dough. Cut off a third of the dough and roll out into a circle the size of the top of the basin, for a lid. Roll out the remainder and line the basin.

Fill the basin with the meat mixture and add sufficient stock to come three quarters of the way up the meat. Damp the edges of the pastry and cover with the lid, sealing firmly. Cover the pudding with a piece of greased greaseproof paper with a pleat in it and a lid of foil. Boil for 3½ to 4 hours, topping up with boiling water when necessary.

The pudding may also be cooked in a pressure cooker. Stand the basin on the trivet and pour in 1½ pints (900 ml) boiling water and a spoonful of vinegar. Seal the cooker, wait for a steady flow of steam and then steam gently for 15 minutes. Raise the heat, bring to 5 lb (2.3 kg) pressure and cook for 1 hour. Then allow the pressure to reduce at room temperature.

SERVES 4

Swiss Steak

A sound family casserole which looks after itself.

PREPARATION AND COOKING TIME: 3½ hours

4 slices topside of beef, each weighing about 6 oz (175 g)
1 tablespoon wholemeal flour
salt
freshly ground black pepper
a little sunflower oil
1 lb (450 g) onions, sliced
6 sticks celery, sliced
14 oz (397 g) can chopped tomatoes
1 tablespoon tomato purée
1 teaspoon Worcestershire sauce

Heat the oven to 325°F/160°C/Gas Mark 3. Cut the slices of beef in half. Mix together the flour and seasoning and toss the meat in the flour, pressing it in so that all the flour is used.

Heat the oil in a pan and fry the meat quickly until browned. Transfer the meat to a fireproof casserole. Add the onion and celery to the fat remaining in the pan and fry gently for about 5 minutes, then add to the meat with the tomatoes, tomato purée and Worcestershire sauce. Bring to the boil and simmer for 5 minutes.

Cover the casserole with a lid and transfer to the oven for about 3 hours, until the meat is tender.

SERVES 4

Boeuf Bourguignonne

A real classic French wine casserole, which is particularly good for winter entertaining.

PREPARATION AND COOKING TIME: 2½ hours

2 lb (900 g) chuck steak
6 oz (150 g) streaky bacon
1 oz (25 g) flour
¼ pint (150 ml) good beef stock
½ pint (300 ml) inexpensive Burgundy
1 bay leaf
scant level teaspoon mixed dried herbs
salt
freshly ground black pepper
12 small pickling onions
6 oz (150 g) button mushrooms
freshly chopped parsley to decorate

Heat the oven to 325°F/160°C/Gas Mark 3. Cut the beef into 1½ inch (4 cm) cubes, and cut the bacon across into small strips. Put the bacon in a pan and heat gently for 3 to 4 minutes until the fat begins to run out, then increase the heat and fry the beef with the bacon strips until browned. Lift out with a slotted spoon and put in a 3 pint (1.7 litre) ovenproof casserole.

Stir the flour into the fat remaining in the pan and cook for a minute. Stir in the stock, wine, bay leaf, herbs and seasoning and bring to the boil, stirring. Pour into the casserole. Cover with a lid or piece of foil and cook in the oven for 1½ hours.

Peel the onions, leave them whole and add to the casserole with the mushrooms. Return to the oven for a further hour, or until the meat is really tender. Taste to check seasoning. Remove the bay leaves and, if necessary, skim off any excess fat. Sprinkle with chopped parsley and serve.

SERVES 6

Pepper-Stuffed Paupiettes

Pre-cooked cracked wheat or bulgar is available in health food shops and some supermarkets. It gives texture to the stuffing and tastes a little like brown rice, but is much easier to prepare. There is no need to tie up the meat rolls – I find that they hold together well if packed together fairly tightly and browned in the oven.

PREPARATION AND COOKING TIME: 4 hours

$1^{1}/_{2}$ oz (40 g) pre-cooked cracked
    wheat (bulgar)
8 thin slices silverside of beef, about
    $2^{1}/_{2}$ lb (1.25 kg) total weight
salt
freshly ground black pepper
1 onion, finely chopped
good knob of butter
1 red pepper, seeded and diced
4 tablespoons freshly chopped
    parsley
a little sunflower oil

RED WINE SAUCE
1 onion, sliced
3 oz (75 g) butter
3 oz (75 g) flour
1 pint (600 ml) red wine
about $^{1}/_{2}$ pint (300 ml) good beef
    stock
salt
freshly ground black pepper

Heat the oven to 450°F/230°C/Gas Mark 8. Cover the cracked wheat with boiling water, leave to stand for 10 minutes, then drain well. Beat out the slices of beef in a polythene bag one at a time, cut in half and season.

Soften the onion in the butter, then add the diced pepper, parsley, seasoning and cracked wheat. Divide the mixture between the slices of beef and roll up carefully. Oil a medium-sized roasting tin, lift the paupiettes into the tin so that the join is underneath and brush the tops with a little oil. Cook the paupiettes near the top of the oven for about 20 minutes, until brown. Drain and save any liquid. Remove from the oven and reduce the temperature to 325°F/160°C/Gas Mark 3.

To make the sauce, soften the onion in the butter, add the flour and cook for a minute, then gradually add the red wine. Make the saved liquid up to a pint (600 ml) with stock, add this to the sauce and bring to the boil, stirring until smooth and slightly thickened. Lift the paupiettes into a large shallow casserole, pour over the sauce and cover. Return to the oven and cook for about 3 hours, or until the beef is tender. Taste and check seasoning, then serve.

SERVES 8

Home-Made Beefburgers

These burgers are very simple to prepare. Serve with salad and a baked potato.

PREPARATION AND COOKING TIME: 30 minutes
CHILLING TIME: 5 hours

8 oz (225 g) onion, chopped
12 oz (350 g) lean minced beef
2 oz (50 g) fresh brown breadcrumbs
1 egg, beaten
2 tablespoons freshly chopped parsley
salt
freshly ground black pepper

Cook the onion in boiling salted water for about 5 minutes until tender, then drain well. Put the onion in a bowl and add the minced beef, breadcrumbs, egg, parsley and seasoning. Mix well until the mixture is thoroughly blended.

Divide the mixture into four. With lightly floured hands, shape the mixture into balls and then flatten to form a burger shape. Chill in the refrigerator for about 5 hours before cooking.

Heat the grill and grill burgers for 10 to 15 minutes, until cooked through, turning once during cooking.

SERVES 4

Baked Meat Loaf

In winter, eat this meat loaf hot with a good thick onion gravy; in summer, bake the loaf and leave it to get quite cold in the tin, then slice thinly and serve with a selection of salads.

PREPARATION AND COOKING TIME: 1¼ hours

2 oz (50 g) fresh brown breadcrumbs
1 medium-sized onion, chopped
¼ level teaspoon chopped fresh herbs
salt
freshly ground black pepper
2 teaspoons Worcestershire sauce
1 level tablespoon tomato ketchup
1 egg
1 lb (450 g) minced beef

Heat the oven to 350°F/180°C/Gas Mark 4. Mix all the ingredients together very thoroughly and turn into a 1 pint (600 ml) loaf tin. Press down firmly and bake in the oven for about 1 hour.

Carefully unmould the meat loaf on to a serving dish.

SERVES 4 to 6

Mozzarella Beef Florentine

This is our favourite mince recipe, served with crusty French bread. Do not keep hot as the spinach then loses colour and the cheese becomes tough. Instead of the Parmesan, you could use 2 oz (50 g) of strong Cheddar cheese.

PREPARATION AND COOKING TIME: 1 hour

2 lb (900 g) lean minced beef
14 oz (397 g) can chopped tomatoes
2 good tablespoons tomato purée
2 cloves garlic, crushed
1 heaped teaspoon sugar
¼ pint (150 ml) good beef stock
salt
freshly ground black pepper
plenty of freshly chopped parsley

SPINACH AND CHEESE FILLING
1½ lb (675 g) washed fresh spinach
knob of butter
2 oz (50 g) fresh white breadcrumbs
2 eggs
salt
freshly ground black pepper
6 oz (175 g) mozzarella cheese,
  thinly sliced
1 oz (25 g) Parmesan cheese, grated

Put the minced beef in a large non-stick pan and cook slowly, breaking down with a wooden spoon until the fat runs out. Then increase the heat and brown the meat. Add the tomatoes, tomato purée, garlic, sugar, stock and seasoning, and bring to the boil, then reduce the heat and simmer, covered, for 45 minutes. Taste and check seasoning.

Meanwhile, make the filling. Just cover the bottom of a large saucepan with water, bring to the boil and cook the spinach until tender (or just thaw the frozen spinach – no need to cook). Drain off any excess liquid and add the butter. Put the breadcrumbs, eggs and seasoning in a bowl and mix very thoroughly, then mix in the spinach.

Heat the oven to 350°F/180°C/Gas Mark 4. Place half the mince in the bottom of a shallow ovenproof dish about 9 by 9 inches (22.5 by 22.5 cm) and cover with the spinach followed by the thinly sliced cheese. Sprinkle on the grated cheese and pour over the remaining mince.

Cover the dish with foil and cook for 30 minutes. Remove the foil and scatter with parsley before serving.

SERVES 4 to 6

Fondue Bourguignonne

Both the Swiss and the French claim this to be one of their traditional dishes, although cheese fondue is probably more Swiss. A fondue party is always a fun idea – particularly as the guests end up cooking their own supper! You will need about 6 oz (175 g) rump steak per person and enough vegetable oil to fill the fondue pot one third full.

Cut the meat into cubes ready to fry in the oil. Have ready skewers, each one marked with coloured tape so that each guest will know which is his.

Heat the oil on the hob of the cooker in the kitchen until a faint haze is rising, then transfer it to the fondue stove. Remember that the oil will heat up more quickly with the lid on the pan, but keep an eye on it because it should not become too hot.

Each guest then inserts his skewer with one or two pieces of meat into the oil until the meat is cooked to his taste. The meat should be taken off the skewers, then speared with a dinner fork, which avoids the chance of lips being burnt.

Keep the oil hot by returning it to the cooker at intervals and try not to cook more than six pieces of meat at a time.

Serve with crisp French bread with butter and a selection of salads, plus a few sauces which may be made in advance.

Curried Mayonnaise Blend 8 tablespoons mayonnaise (*page 152*) with juice of ½ lemon, 2 teaspoons curry powder and 2 tablespoons very finely chopped mango chutney.

Mustard and Dill Blend 8 tablespoons mayonnaise (*page 152*) with 2 tablespoons Dijon mustard and 1 teaspoon chopped dill.

Chutney Blend 8 tablespoons mayonnaise (*page 152*) with chopped chunky tomato chutney or just serve tomato chutney on its own.

Egg and Parsley Blend 8 tablespoons mayonnaise (*page 152*) with 2 finely chopped hard-boiled eggs and 2 tablespoons freshly chopped parsley.

North Indian Curry

This recipe was given by me by Fatima Lakhani as a curry that her family has enjoyed for generations. It is not overpoweringly strong, has a superb flavour and rich colour and is surprisingly simple to make. Instead of mixing the spices yourself, you can use 3 rounded tablespoons curry powder.

PREPARATION AND COOKING TIME: 3 hours

2 rounded tablespoons ground coriander
1 rounded teaspoon ground cummin
1 level teaspoon ground turmeric
1 rounded teaspoon garam masala
2 fat cloves garlic, crushed
piece fresh green ginger the size of a walnut, finely chopped
salt
3 tablespoons sunflower oil
2 large onions, chopped
8 oz (227 g) can chopped tomatoes
2 generous tablespoons tomato purée
2 lb (900 g) chuck steak, cut into cubes
½ pint (300 ml) water
fresh mango slices to garnish
a little lemon juice

First mix the spices together, then add the garlic, ginger and salt. Take a heavy pan, measure in the oil, add the onions and fry until an even golden brown. (Do not let them catch and brown as this would spoil the flavour.) Add the spice mixture, tomatoes and tomato purée, and cook over a medium heat, stirring, until the oil starts to come through slightly. Then add the meat, cover with a lid and simmer for 15 minutes. Remove the lid and add the water. Bring to the boil, cover and simmer gently for about 2½ hours, or until the meat is tender.

Garnish the curry with fresh mango slices, brushed with lemon juice to prevent discoloration.

SERVES 6

Curry Accompaniments

These are a vital part of an Indian meal. Rice and poppodums are the first essentials, then a variety of sambols or side dishes can be served as well.

Rice   Use basmati rice or long-grain American rice. Allow about 2 oz (50 g) rice per person and cook in plenty of salted water until just tender. Indian pilau rice bought in packets is a yellow spiced saffron rice and adds variety. Rice is quite easy to reheat: it can either be put in a buttered dish, covered with foil with a few holes in the top and reheated gently in a slow oven, or plunged into a pan of boiling salted water for about 2 minutes to heat through, then drained and served.

Poppodums   These are easily available nowadays in a variety of flavours. They are deep-fat fried, drained well, and then served in a tall pile on the table. Some poppodums can be crisped under the grill.

Onion and Green Pepper   Thinly slice a mild onion and mix with finely sliced strips of green pepper. I like to skin the pepper before slicing it: stand it under a hot grill for about 2 minutes, then the skin will peel off easily.

Banana   Slice a couple of bananas and toss in lemon juice to prevent them from discolouring.

Cucumber, Mint and Yoghurt   Dice a 3 inch (2.75 cm) long piece of cucumber and stir into ¼ pint (150 ml) natural yoghurt with a tablespoon of freshly chopped mint. Season to taste with salt and pepper.

Chutney and Pickles   I always cheat with these and buy them ready-made. Mango chutney and lime and brinjal (aubergine) pickles are the best.

Royal Lamb Curry

The flavour of this curry is divine. The recipe was given to me by Khalid Aziz and I have adapted it slightly. Serve with rice and a selection of sambols (*page 77*).

PREPARATION AND COOKING TIME: 1¼ hours

2 lb (900 g) lean shoulder lamb
¾ pint (450 ml) good stock
1 small piece cinnamon stick
2 bay leaves
rind and juice of 1 small lemon
2 fat cloves garlic, crushed
1 teaspoon ground cardamom
½ teaspoon ground cloves
1 tablespoon ground coriander
2 tablespoons sunflower oil
1 large onion, chopped
salt
freshly ground black pepper
2 oz (50 g) split almonds
2 oz (50 g) raisins
½ pint (300 ml) Greek yoghurt

Cut the lamb into 1 inch (2.5 cm) cubes and put it in a pan with the stock, cinnamon, bay leaves and lemon rind and juice. Bring to the boil then cover with a lid and simmer gently for about 30 minutes. Lift out the meat with a slotted spoon and boil the remaining liquid rapidly until reduced by half. Add the garlic, cardamom, cloves and coriander and stir well.

Heat the oil in a large pan and fry the onion until soft, then add the lamb and fry quickly for a minute. Strain the reduced stock, add it to the pan with the salt and pepper, and simmer gently for about 30 minutes. Stir in the almonds, raisins and yoghurt, and continue cooking for about 5 minutes.

SERVES 6

Moussaka

Use minced shoulder of lamb, but be sure to drain off all surplus fat after frying it, otherwise the dish could be fatty. I now never fry the aubergines first, for the same reason. Serve with a mixed salad.

PREPARATION AND COOKING TIME: 1 hour

1 lb (450 g) minced lamb
8 oz (225 g) onions, sliced
2 fat cloves garlic, crushed
1 oz (25 g) flour
salt
freshly ground black pepper
14 oz (397 g) can chopped
*   tomatoes*
2 aubergines

CHEESE SAUCE
1 oz (25 g) butter
1 oz (25 g) flour
½ pint (300 ml) milk
1 teaspoon Dijon mustard
a little grated nutmeg
salt
freshly ground black pepper
3 oz (75 g) Cheddar cheese, grated
1 egg, beaten

Cook the lamb in a non-stick pan over a low heat to let the fat run out, then drain and add the onions and garlic. Increase the heat and fry quickly until the meat is browned. Stir in the flour, seasoning and tomatoes, bring to the boil and simmer for about 5 minutes.

Slice the aubergines and blanch in boiling salted water for about 1 minute to soften the skins and stop discoloration. Drain dry on kitchen paper.

To make the sauce, melt the butter in a pan then stir in the flour and cook for about 1 minute. Gradually blend in milk and bring to the boil, stirring well. Add the mustard, nutmeg, seasoning and cheese. Remove from heat and stir in egg when cooled slightly. Mix well.

To assemble the moussaka, spread half the meat mixture over the bottom of a large, greased ovenproof dish, cover with half the aubergines, season and repeat with remaining meat and aubergines. Pour over the cheese sauce.

Cook the moussaka, uncovered, at 350°F/180°C/Gas Mark 4 for 45 minutes to an hour, until golden brown.

SERVES 6

Irish Stew

Although a true Irish stew has no carrots, we prefer them added. It's a perfect dish for a wintry day.

PREPARATION AND COOKING TIME: 2¼ hours

8 middle neck lamb chops
1 lb (450 g) onions, sliced
2 lb (900 g) potatoes, sliced
salt
freshly ground black pepper
8 oz (225 g) carrots, sliced
water

Heat the oven to 325°F/160°C/Gas Mark 3. Trim any excess fat off lamb. Put half the onion into a 3 pint (1.7 litre) casserole, add half the potato and then the meat, seasoning each layer well. Cover with the carrots, then add the remaining onion and finish with a layer of potato. Add enough water to come half way up the casserole.

Cover and cook in the oven for about an hour, then remove the lid and cook for a further hour.

SERVES 4

Honey-Glazed Lamb

To me it is a real joy to put a roast in the oven and for it to come out ready to serve, with the delicious gravy cum sauce made in the roasting tin underneath. This is a top family favourite. Sometimes I used boned leg of lamb opened out like a butterfly instead of loin of lamb. It takes longer to cook – about 55 minutes for a good sized boned leg. I add the marinade half way through in the same way as in the recipe below.

PREPARATION AND COOKING TIME: 40 minutes
MARINATING TIME: at least 12 hours

best end and loin of lamb in a piece, sawn through
the chine into 12 chops

MARINADE
8 fl oz (250 ml) orange juice
3 tablespoons clear honey
3 tablespoons soy sauce
2 cloves garlic, crushed
2 heaped teaspoons dried rosemary
1 teaspoon ground ginger

Combine all the ingredients for the marinade. Take two large freezer bags and put one inside the other, then put the lamb and the marinade into the bag, seal and leave for at least 12 hours in the refrigerator, turning occasionally. (The lamb may be left to marinate for up to 3 days.)

Heat the oven to 450°F/230°C/Gas Mark 8. Reserving the marinade, place the lamb in a roasting tin and roast for 20 minutes. Pour over the marinade and cook for a further 10 to 15 minutes, until the marinade has changed colour and become a dark gravy, and when the lamb is pierced with a skewer the juices run clear.

To serve, cut through the bones to give two chops each. Skim off any fat from the gravy and serve the gravy with the chops.

SERVES 6

Lemon Lamb Fricassee

Do try to use fresh thyme, preferably lemon thyme – this is very easy to grow and once planted it goes on for years. Serve with mashed potatoes to sop up the wonderful velvety sauce.

PREPARATION AND COOKING TIME: 2¼ hours

2 lb (900 g) boneless shoulder lamb, cubed
a little sunflower oil
1½ oz (40 g) flour
4 fl oz (120 ml) white wine
3 cloves garlic, crushed
1 pint (600 ml) good chicken stock
thinly peeled rind and juice of 2 lemons
salt
freshly ground black pepper
3 generous sprigs thyme
2 egg yolks
a little freshly chopped parsley

Heat the oven to 325°F/160°C/Gas Mark 3. Heat a little oil in a non-stick pan and brown the lamb, a little at a time. Transfer to a fireproof casserole, using a slotted spoon. Sprinkle the flour on to the meat, stir and cook for about a minute. Add the wine and garlic, then the stock, a little at a time. Add the lemon zest and 2 of the sprigs of thyme, season and bring to the boil, stirring until thickened. Simmer for 5 minutes.

Cover the casserole and transfer to the oven for about an hour, or until the lamb is tender. Drain off and reserve the liquid, and throw away the lemon zest and sprigs of thyme.

Strip the leaves off the remaining sprig of thyme. Blend together the lemon juice and egg yolks. Bring the reserved liquid to the boil, add a little of the hot liquid to the lemon and yolks, mix well and return to the pan. Whisking well, bring just to the boil, then add the thyme leaves. Pour the sauce over the meat and return to the oven for about 20 minutes.

Before serving, skim off any excess fat, check seasoning and sprinkle with parsley.

SERVES 6

Rutland Lamb

If you like your lamb pink, reduce the cooking time as follows: slice the onions thinly and cook the lamb at 350°F/180°C/Gas Mark 4 for 20 minutes to the pound (450 g), uncovering the lamb half way through.

PREPARATION AND COOKING TIME: 2¼ hours

1 leg of English lamb
4 slices ham
2 cloves garlic, crushed
1 teaspoon dried rosemary
freshly ground black pepper
2 large onions, sliced
1 glass white wine
salt
parsley to garnish

Using a sharp knife, bone the lamb, leaving the shank bone in place (or get the butcher to do this for you). Heat the oven to 350°F/180°C/Gas Mark 4.

Spread the slices of ham with the crushed garlic and sprinkle with some of the rosemary and pepper. Roll up and stuff into the lamb in place of the bone.

Place the onions in a large casserole and lay the leg of lamb on top. Pour over the wine and sprinkle with the remaining rosemary. Season well. Cover with a lid or a piece of foil and cook for 35 minutes per pound (450 g) plus 35 minutes over. After an hour, lower the oven temperature to 325°F/160°C/Gas Mark 3 and remove the lid for the remaining cooking time.

Serve the onions and juices with the meat. Garnish with parsley.

SERVES 6 to 8

Kashmir Lamb

Sometimes fillet of neck of lamb is hard to come by so use lean shoulder of lamb instead. Serve with rice and a green salad with freshly chopped mint. If you like a lot of sauce, add extra yoghurt.

PREPARATION AND COOKING TIME: 2 hours

1½ lb (675 g) fillet of neck of lamb
2 tablespoons sunflower oil
1 large onion, chopped
2 fat cloves garlic, crushed
1 teaspoon ground turmeric
1 teaspoon ground cummin
1 teaspoon ground coriander
1 level tablespoon flour
¼ pint (150 ml) good chicken stock
salt
freshly ground black pepper
¼ pint (150 ml) natural yoghurt

Cut the fillet into discs the thickness of thick sliced bread. Measure the oil into a large pan, brown the meat on both sides then lift out with a slotted spoon into a small casserole.

Fry the onion in the oil remaining in the pan and add the garlic. Stir in the spices and flour and cook for a minute, then gradually blend in the stock and bring to the boil, stirring until thickened. Season and pour over the meat. Cover with a lid or a piece of foil.

Place the casserole in the oven at 325°F/160°C/Gas Mark 3 and cook for 1 to 1½ hours, or until the meat is tender. Stir in the yoghurt and mix well. Serve straight away, without reboiling.

SERVES 4

Grilled Noisettes of Lamb

These tiny chops look very special and can be prepared in advance, then just slipped under the grill. If you prefer not to use bacon, leave a little more fat on the chop.

PREPARATION AND COOKING TIME: 30 minutes

8 loin of lamb chops in the piece, about 1½ lb (675 g) total weight
4 lamb's kidneys
salt
freshly ground black pepper
8 thin long streaky bacon rashers

First bone the lamb. With a very sharp knife remove the skin with some of the fat from the outer side, then carefully run the knife down close to the bone to remove ribs and backbone. Take out any gristle or extra fat and divide into eight long strips, each with an eye of lean meat.

Remove the skin from the kidneys, core them and cut each in half. Season the kidneys and meat. Take each boned chop, lay it on its side and put half a kidney next to the eye of meat, then wrap the long strip of rather fatty meat round the outside. Wrap a piece of bacon round each chop and secure with a wooden cocktail stick.

Grill under a moderate grill for 8 to 10 minutes, turning once, until when pierced with a fine skewer the juices that flow are just clear.

SERVES 4

Crisp Roast Pork with Apples

An easy to carve roast good for entertaining. Get the butcher to bone the loin for you, and use the bones to make stock. Also, have the crackling finely scored by the butcher.

PREPARATION AND COOKING TIME: 2¼ hours

3½ lb (1.6 kg) joint loin pork,
    boned, crackling left on
2 pig's kidneys
8 oz (225 g) pork sausagemeat
1 tablespoon chopped parsley
1 teaspoon rubbed dried sage
salt
freshly ground black pepper
a little oil

GLAZED APPLES
4 Cox's apples
2 tablespoons demerara sugar
1 oz (25 g) butter

Heat oven to 350°F/180°C/Gas Mark 4. Remove the skin from the kidneys and snip out the core with sharp scissors or a knife. Mix the sausagemeat with the herbs and seasoning.

Lay the joint skin side down on a board. With a very sharp knife, remove any pieces of white tough skin where the rib bones were, season lightly and spread with the sausagemeat. Lay the kidneys side by side lengthways on the sausagemeat.

Fold the joint over the stuffing and secure with about three skewers, or with string. Turn over on to a piece of foil and lift into a roasting tin with the crackling uppermost. Rub with a little oil, sprinkle with salt and roast for about 2 hours, until the crackling is crisp and when the meat is prodded with a fine skewer the juices that run out are clear.

Just before serving, prepare the apples. Core them, leaving the skin on, cut into thickish slices to make rings and toss in the demerara sugar. Melt the butter in a frying pan and quickly brown the apples. Serve with the pork and a thin gravy made from the meat juices.

SERVES 6 to 8

Justin Pork Chops

An unusual and surprisingly simple supper dish. Work over a bowl when you prepare the oranges so that none of the juice is wasted.

PREPARATION AND COOKING TIME: 50 minutes

4 lean pork chops
Dijon mustard
about 4 oz (100 g) light muscovado sugar
2 small oranges, segmented, all pips and pith removed

Trim the chops of excess fat and spread with mustard on both sides. Roll the chops in sugar until well coated, then lay them in a greased shallow oven-proof dish. Arrange the orange segments on top of the chops and pour over any juice you have collected while segmenting them.

Bake, uncovered, at 375°F/190°C/Gas Mark 5 for about 45 minutes, until the chops are tender, basting occasionally. Serve with the juices as a gravy.

SERVES 4

Ginger Spiced Pork

This recipe is a real top favourite. Add more Tabasco if you like it hot.

PREPARATION AND COOKING TIME: 2½ hours

2 tablespoons oil
knob of butter
2 lb (900 kg) lean shoulder of pork, cubed
2 level tablespoons brown sugar
1 oz (25 g) flour
2 level teaspoons ground ginger
14 oz (397 g) can chopped tomatoes
4 oz (100 g) button mushrooms
2 tablespoons vinegar
2 cloves garlic, crushed
1 tablespoon Worcestershire sauce
dash of Tabasco sauce
salt
freshly ground black pepper

Heat the oven to 325°F/160°C/Gas Mark 3. Measure the oil into a large frying pan, add the butter and fry the meat until all moisture has been driven off and the meat is almost beginning to brown. Add the sugar and toss over a high heat until brown. Add the flour and ginger to the pan and blend well, then add the remaining ingredients. Stir until the sauce thickens.

Transfer to a casserole, cover and cook in the oven for about 2 hours, or until the meat is tender. Check seasoning before serving.

SERVES 6

Sweet and Sour Spare Rib Chops

Spare rib chops are cheaper than loin chops and very good served this way.
Trim off any excess fat before browning them.

PREPARATION AND COOKING TIME: 1¼ hours

4 large or 8 small spare rib chops
1 rounded tablespoon apricot jam
1 teaspoon Dijon mustard
good pinch cayenne pepper
1 fat clove garlic, crushed
1 tablespoon Worcestershire sauce
3 tablespoons tomato ketchup
1 tablespoon soy sauce
salt
freshly ground black pepper

Heat the oven to 350°F/180°C/Gas Mark 4. Put the chops in a non-stick pan
and fry gently until the fat begins to run, then increase the heat and fry
quickly for about 10 minutes, until browned all over. Lift the chops into a
shallow ovenproof dish and arrange so that they just touch.

Mix together the jam, mustard, cayenne pepper, garlic and Worcestershire
sauce until blended, then stir in the remaining ingredients. Pour the sauce
over the chops, coating them evenly. Cover with a piece of foil.

Cook in the oven for about an hour, until the meat is tender.

SERVES 4

Norfolk Hotpot

This hotpot takes time to make but is so good. If the bacon stock is on the salty side, use a stock cube and water instead in the sauce. A knuckle of fore-hock of bacon is one of the cheaper cuts.

PREPARATION AND COOKING TIME: 3¾ hours

1 knuckle of forehock of bacon
1 bay leaf
1 lb (450 g) onions, sliced
1 lb (450 g) potatoes, peeled and sliced
2 oz (50 g) butter
2 oz (50 g) flour
¾ pint (450 ml) milk
¾ pint (450 ml) stock from the bacon
salt
freshly ground black pepper

Soak the knuckle in a pan of cold water overnight then throw away the water. Cover knuckle with fresh water and add the bay leaf. Put the lid on the pan, bring to the boil, and simmer gently for about 2 hours or until tender. Lift the knuckle out of the stock and allow to cool. When cool, take the meat off the bone and discard the skin, fat and bones. Cut the meat into small cubes.

Bring a large pan of salted water to the boil, add the onions and potatoes and simmer for about 10 minutes. Drain and put about 15 of the largest slices of potato aside to cover the casserole.

Heat the oven to 375°F/190°C/Gas Mark 5. Melt the butter in a pan, stir in the flour and cook for 1 minute. Gradually blend in the milk and stock and stir until thickened. Mix the sauce with the bacon, onion and potato (except for the reserved slices), check seasoning, then pour into a 3 pint (1.7 litre) casserole. Top with the reserved slices of potato and put the hotpot in the oven and cook, covered, for about an hour. Remove the lid for the last 30 minutes of cooking time.

SERVES 6

POULTRY AND GAME

Chicken is a wonderful buy – the least expensive and one of the most versatile of meats – and included here are many recipes for breasts and joints of chicken. Duck breasts are available now, too, and unlike the rest of the duck they have plenty of meat on them.

Pheasant is perhaps the one meat that really improves with freezing – just make sure that it is well wrapped. If you want more of a budget dish, use the same recipe and substitute pigeon.

Chicken in Tarragon Cream

This sauce for cold chicken is wonderful. If left in the refrigerator overnight, the flavours will have time to develop and penetrate the chicken.

PREPARATION AND COOKING TIME: 5 minutes
CHILLING TIME: overnight

1 lb (500 g) cold cooked chicken, cut into manageable pieces
watercress sprigs to garnish

SAUCE
2 spring onions
1 teaspoon chopped fresh tarragon
1 teaspoon chopped fresh chervil
1 good tablespoon caster sugar
2 egg yolks
1 teaspoon Dijon mustard
1 oz (25 g) canned anchovy fillets, cut into thin slivers
6 tablespoons sunflower oil
4 tablespoons tarragon or white wine vinegar
¼ pint (150 ml) whipping cream, whipped
salt
freshly ground black pepper

Measure all the sauce ingredients into a large bowl and blend together thoroughly. Taste and check seasoning then add the chicken and mix well.

Turn into a serving dish and leave in the refrigerator overnight to chill. Serve garnished with a few sprigs of watercress.

SERVES 6

Cheese and Pineapple Chicken

Cheese and pineapple are an excellent combination, but an unusual one to cook with chicken. I was doubtful when it was recommended to me but now I rate it highly, being easy to prepare and going down well with all ages. This dish freezes well, too.

PREPARATION AND COOKING TIME: 1 hour

2 tablespoons sunflower oil
2 oz (50 g) butter
6 chicken joints, skinned
1 medium-sized onion, sliced
2 oz (50 g) flour
about ¾ pint (450 ml) good chicken stock
15 oz (425 g) can pineapple pieces in natural juice
8 oz (225 g) well-flavoured Cheddar cheese, grated
salt
freshly ground black pepper

Heat the oven to 350°F/180°C/Gas Mark 4. Measure the oil and butter into a large pan and fry the chicken for about 10 minutes, until golden brown. Lift out of the pan with a slotted spoon and arrange in a large ovenproof dish.

Add the onion to the juices left in the pan and cook for about 5 minutes, until soft. Sprinkle in the flour and cook for a minute, then gradually blend in the stock and the juice from the can of pineapple. Bring to the boil, stirring until thickened, then remove from the heat and stir in the pineapple pieces, three quarters of the cheese and seasoning to taste.

Pour the sauce over the chicken, sprinkle with the remaining cheese and cook in the oven for about 40 minutes, until the chicken is tender and the cheese has melted and is golden brown. Serve at once.

SERVES 6

Badminton Chicken

So called because at short notice we decided to go to one of the three-day events. I had already roasted a large chicken for the weekend, but I wanted to make it more special and manageable to eat with a fork, knowing we would either be standing up or balancing a plate while sitting on a rug. Preparing it the night before was ideal, as the mild spicy flavour really penetrated the chicken. The recipe is not unlike the cordon bleu Coronation Chicken, but the sauce is made in a few minutes! A good accompaniment is Green Salad with Fennel (*page 146*).

PREPARATION AND COOKING TIME: 15 minutes
CHILLING TIME: overnight

1 cold roast chicken, weighing about 4 lb (1.8 kg)
¾ pint (450 ml) mayonnaise (page 152)
2 tablespoons tomato purée
6 tablespoons mango chutney
2 tablespoons lemon juice
1 heaped teaspoon curry powder
salt
freshly ground black pepper
1 fresh mango, peeled and sliced, to decorate
freshly chopped parsley

Take all the skin off the bird, remove the bones and cut the meat into manageable pieces.

Measure the mayonnaise, tomato purée, chutney and lemon juice into a bowl, cutting up any large pieces in the mango chutney. Add the curry powder and season well, then taste and add more curry powder if necessary. Add the chicken, cover and chill overnight in the refrigerator.

The next day, pile into a shallow serving dish, decorate with mango slices and sprinkle parsley over the top.

SERVES 8

Barbecue Chicken Drumsticks

These are always taken on all our family picnics. The children set to and make them for me just in case I run short of time – they enjoy the scrapings from the roasting tin at the end. Sometimes I use chicken thighs which are more meaty but more difficult to eat in the fingers. This recipe can be cooked over charcoal on the barbecue instead of in the oven, and will then need basting often with the sauce.

PREPARATION AND COOKING TIME: 45 minutes

12 chicken drumsticks

SAUCE
3 tablespoons sunflower oil
3 tablespoons vinegar
2 tablespoons tomato ketchup
1 tablespoon Worcestershire sauce
dash of Tabasco sauce
2 level tablespoons dark brown sugar
salt
freshly ground black pepper
1 small onion, quartered
1 fat clove garlic, crushed

Heat the oven to 425°F/220°C/Gas Mark 7. Measure all the sauce ingredients in a processor or blender, and process until the smooth. Arrange the drumsticks in a single layer in roasting tin. Spoon over sauce and cook until a deep golden colour, basting once or twice. (This will take bout 35 minutes.)

Leave the drumsticks to cool a little, then wrap the boney ends in foil so that they can be picked up easily. Arrange on a dish, foil ends outwards.

SERVES 6

Eastern Stir-Fry

It helps to chill the chicken before you slice it into strips.

PREPARATION AND COOKING TIME: 15 minutes

12 oz (350 g) skinless chicken breast fillets
12 oz (350 g) white cabbage
6 spring onions
2 level teaspoons cornflour
2 tablespoons sherry
2 tablespoons sunflower oil
salt
freshly ground black pepper
1 red pepper, seeded and sliced
12 oz (350 g) bean sprouts
1 clove garlic, crushed
⅛ pint (75 ml) good chicken stock
2 tablespoons soy sauce

Slice the chicken into pencil-thin strips. Shred the cabbage finely. Cut each spring onion into three. Blend the cornflour with the sherry.

Heat the oil in a wok or large frying pan until very hot. Season the chicken and cook for 2 minutes, stirring all the time. Lift out with a slotted spoon and set to one side.

Reheat the pan and add the cabbage, red pepper, bean sprouts, spring onions and garlic. Cook for 3 to 4 minutes, stirring all the time. Return the chicken to the pan and stir in the stock, soy sauce and sherry mixture. Cook for a further minute until the liquid has thickened slightly and the vegetables are stil crisp. Taste and check seasoning, and serve at once.

SERVES 4

RIGHT: *Crisp Roast Pork with Apples (page 86)*

Saturday Chicken

So easy – the stuffing thickens the sauce and imparts a herby flavour. If you have no wine to hand, you could use cider.

PREPARATION AND COOKING TIME: 1¼ hours

2 tablespoons sunflower oil
4 leg portions roasting chicken, skinned
2 rounded tablespoons lemon and thyme stuffing mix
1 large clove garlic, crushed
14 oz (397 g) can chopped tomatoes
1 chicken stock cube
¼ pint (150 ml) red wine
1 good tablespoon apricot or other seedless jam
salt
freshly ground black pepper

Heat the oven to 350°F/180°C/Gas Mark 4. Heat the oil in a frying pan and fry the chicken so that it is brown on all sides. Lift out the chicken and put it in a casserole.

Measure all the other ingredients into the frying pan, and stir well to incorporate any sediment and melt the jam. Pour over the chicken, cover the casserole and cook in the oven for about 1 hour, until the chicken is tender. Taste and check seasoning before serving.

SERVES 4

LEFT: *Eastern Stir-Fry (page 96)*

Chicken and Tarragon Raised Pie

The pastry for this pie is very easy to make and is lovely and crisp. It is a nice change from the more usual shortcrust.

PREPARATION AND COOKING TIME: 1¾ hours
CHILLING TIME: overnight

*1 chicken, weighing about 3½ lb
   (1.6 kg)*
8 oz (225 g) pork sausagemeat
1 tablespoon chopped fresh tarragon
1 teaspoon ground mace
2 teaspoons salt
freshly ground black pepper
*8 oz (225 g) ham, cut into long thin
   strips*
*6 small hard-boiled eggs, shelled
   and with the white trimmed from
   each end so that the yolk is just
   showing through*
beaten egg and milk to glaze

PASTRY
12 oz (350 g) plain flour
1 teaspoon salt
5 oz (150 g) lard
6 fl oz (175 ml) water

Heat the oven to 425°F/220°C/Gas Mark 7 and grease a 2 lb (1.2 kg) loaf tin.

Carve off the legs and thighs from the raw chicken, then remove the skin and bones. Take the meat off the rest of the bird. Cube all the chicken and put it in a bowl with the sausagemeat, tarragon, mace and seasonings.

To make the pastry, put the flour and salt in a bowl. Place the lard and water in a pan and allow the water to boil and the lard to melt. Make a well in the centre of the flour and pour in all the liquid, mixing quickly with a wooden spoon until it becomes a smooth dough.

When cool enough to handle, take two thirds of the dough and work it round the inside and up the sides of the prepared tin. Arrange half the ham in the bottom of the tin, followed by half the meat mixture. Make six dents in the mixture and arrange the eggs end to end along the length of the tin. Cover with the remaining meat mixture and ham.

Knead the remaining pastry into an oblong big enough to cover the top of the pie, press the edges firmly together and flute or just press with the prongs of a fork. Make four small holes in the top of the pie and decorate with pastry leaves. Brush the pie with beaten egg and milk and cook in the oven for 45 minutes, then reduce the heat to 350°F/180°C/Gas Mark 4 for a further 30 minutes.

Leave the pie to cool in the tin, then chill overnight before turning out on to a serving plate.

SERVES 10

Chicken in Cider with Mushrooms

An untemperamental dish, easy to serve when friends are in for a meal. Sometimes I omit the mushrooms and add a can of drained red peppers, sliced. I save a few slices of pepper to decorate the chicken with a criss-cross diagonal pattern which really looks stunning. I always make it ahead then reheat when I need it. It freezes well, too.

PREPARATION AND COOKING TIME: 1¾ hours

1 chicken, weighing about 3½ lb (1.6 kg)
½ pint (300 ml) dry cider
1 onion, chopped
salt
freshly ground black pepper
1 pint (600 ml) milk
2 oz (50 g) butter
2 oz (50 g) flour
8 oz (225 g) button mushrooms, sliced
croûtons of fried bread (page 103) to garnish
chopped parsley

Heat the oven to 350°F/180°C/Gas Mark 4. Put the chicken and giblets in a small roasting tin or casserole, add the cider and onion and season well. Cover with a lid or a piece of foil and cook in the oven for about 1½ hours. Test to see if it is cooked by piercing the thickest part of the leg with a skewer; if the juices come out clear, the bird is cooked. Lift the chicken out to cool. Strain off the remaining liquid in the tin, skim off the fat and make up to 1¼ pints (750 ml) with milk.

Remove the meat from the bird and cut into good-sized pieces. Chop the chicken liver and add it to the meat. (The remaining giblets and carcass can be used to make stock for soup on another occasion.)

Melt the butter in a pan, add the flour and cook for 2 minutes without colouring. Stir in the stock and milk, slowly at first, and bring to the boil, then add the mushrooms and season with salt and lots of black pepper. Stir in the chicken and turn into a serving dish. Sprinkle with chopped parsley and serve garnished with coûtons of fried bread.

SERVES 6

Devilled Chicken

What are we having tonight, Mum? Well, this is very often the answer when (1) I haven't thought, and (2) I haven't been shopping! I usually have chicken joints in the freezer as a standby, and the rest of the ingredients are always in the cupboard. I've made this recipe since the children were small and it is even more popular now than it was then.

PREPARATION AND COOKING TIME: 1¼ hours

4 thigh roasting joints of chicken
salt
freshly ground black pepper
1 rounded tablespoon apricot jam
1 teaspoon Dijon mustard
pinch cayenne pepper
large clove garlic, crushed
1 tablespoon Worcestershire sauce
3 tablespoons tomato ketchup
1 tablespoon soy sauce

Heat the oven to 350°F/180°C/Gas Mark 4. Season the chicken joints well on all sides and arrange in a shallow ovenproof dish so that they just touch.

Measure the jam into a basin, add the mustard, cayenne, garlic and Worcestershire sauce, and blend well until smooth. Add the other ingredients, season with black pepper and a little salt, and pour over the chicken joints, coating them evenly.

Bake for about 1 hour at the top of the oven. If the juices that run out when the thickest part of a thigh is prodded with a fork are clear, the chicken is done; if pink, cook for a little longer.

SERVES 4

Chicken à la Crème

Some of the simplest recipes are the best. The important point is not to over-cook the chicken breasts: they should still feel springy when cooked. If in doubt, make a slit in the centre of one of the breasts (the sauce will cover it afterwards) and take off the heat when only a hint of pink blood is left. By the time the chicken has been kept warm for serving and covered with the hot sauce, it will be cooked through but not toughened. As a variation, try Mustard Chicken: omit the mushrooms and instead add a good tablespoon of Dijon mustard just before serving the sauce. Very good with broccoli.

PREPARATION AND COOKING TIME: 20 minutes

4 chicken breasts, skinned and boned
1 oz (25 g) butter
1 tablespoon sunflower oil
8 oz (225 g) button mushrooms, sliced
¼ pint (150 ml) white wine
½ pint (300 ml) double cream
salt
freshly ground black pepper
freshly chopped parsley

Trim the chicken, if necessary. Measure the butter and oil into a large frying pan and fry the chicken for 2 to 3 minutes on each side until golden brown and just done (see note above). Remove the chicken breasts to a serving dish and keep warm.

Add the mushrooms to the pan, toss over heat for 1 minute, then lift out with a slotted spoon on to a plate. Pour the wine and any juices that have drained from the chicken into the pan. Reduce the liquid by half over a high heat, add the cream and cook to a creamy sauce. Return the mushrooms to the pan, season and pour over the chicken breasts. Sprinkle with parsley to serve.

SERVES 4

Chicken Marengo

A sound French casserole, served with croûtons of fried bread. To make these, use slices of brown or white bread cut into triangles and fry on both sides until crisp. Use them to decorate the chicken, but take care not to let them sink into the sauce or they will go soggy.

PREPARATION AND COOKING TIME: 1 hour

2 tablespoons sunflower oil
1 oz (25 g) butter
6 chicken joints
1 oz (25 g) flour
½ pint (300 ml) dry white wine or cider
¼ pint (150 ml) good chicken stock
14 oz (397 g) can chopped tomatoes
salt
freshly ground black pepper
1 clove garlic, crushed
6 oz (175 g) button mushrooms
croûtons of fried bread to decorate

Heat the oil and butter in a large frying pan and fry the chicken quickly until brown on both sides. Lift out and set to one side. Add the flour to the pan and cook for a minute or two, then stir in the wine and stock and bring to the boil, stirring until thickened. Add the tomatoes, seasoning and garlic, then return the chicken to the pan. Cover and simmer for 30 minutes.

Add the mushrooms (leave them whole) and continue cooking for a further 15 minutes, or until the chicken is tender. Test by prodding with a fork – if the juices run clear, the chicken is cooked. Taste and check seasoning.

Arrange the chicken on a warm serving dish and spoon over the sauce. Decorate with croûtons of fried bread.

SERVES 6

English Hot Chicken Salad

A lighter way of serving chicken – a top favourite as a summer lunch.

PREPARATION AND COOKING TIME: 15 minutes

4 oz (100 g) mild streaky bacon, snipped in pieces
3 oz (75 g) flaked almonds
salt
freshly ground black pepper
4 chicken breasts, skinned and boned and cut into
  ½ inch (1.25 cm) strips
chopped parsley

SALAD
1 crisp lettuce
1 bunch watercress
6 tablespoons French dressing (page 153)

First prepare the salad: break the lettuce into manageable-sized pieces and trim the watercress stalks.

Put bacon into a non-stick frying pan and cook slowly until the fat begins to run, then increase the heat and fry until nearly crisp. Add the almonds and allow to brown. Lift the bacon and almonds out of the pan with a slotted spoon and keep warm.

Season the chicken and cook quickly in the same pan for about 5 minutes, tossing to brown all sides. Return the bacon and almonds to the pan for a moment.

Toss the salad in French dressing and divide between four plates. Top with the chicken, bacon and almonds, sprinkle with parsley and serve.

SERVES 4

American Hot Chicken Salad

This highly successful recipe has been served to hundreds for high days and holidays. It is very easy and quick. The recipe originally had 2 tablespoons chopped onion, but I prefer to add 4 finely sliced spring onions. Best served with brown French bread and Green Salad with Fennel (*page 146*).

PREPARATION AND COOKING TIME: 20 minutes

12 oz (350 g) cooked chicken or turkey, diced
4 sticks celery, sliced
4 spring onions, finely sliced
1/2 pint (300 ml) mayonnaise (page 152)
2 teaspoons lemon juice
4 oz (100 g) well-flavoured Cheddar cheese, grated
salt
freshly ground black pepper
a few potato crisps, crumbled
a little paprika

Heat the oven to 425°F/220°C/Gas Mark 7. Measure the chicken, celery, spring onions, mayonnaise and lemon juice into a bowl, together with 3 oz (75 g) of the cheese. Season and blend together, then turn the mixture into a shallow ovenproof dish. Top with the remaining cheese, the crisps and a dusting of paprika.

Cook in the oven for 12 to 15 minutes, until hot but not boiling. Don't cook any longer, otherwise the sauce will separate. Serve straight away.

SERVES 4

Roast Poussin with Garlic Potatoes

A special dish for a special occasion. Poussins vary in size from 12 oz (350 g) – enough for one each – to double that weight. Split a large poussin in half through the breastbone with a sharp knife to serve two.

PREPARATION AND COOKING TIME: 1 hour

12 oz (350 g) peeled potatoes
a little flour
knob of butter
1 tablespoon sunflower oil
1 clove garlic, crushed
salt
freshly ground black pepper
2 poussins

Heat the oven to 400°F/200°C/Gas Mark 6. Cut the potatoes into cubes the size of large sugar lumps. Put in a pan and cover with cold water, bring to the boil for one minute, then drain. Dust the potatoes with flour. Grease a shallow dish about 8 inches (20 cm) across with the butter, then add the oil and garlic and season well.

Put the potatoes in the dish and lay the poussins on top, covering the breasts with pieces of buttered paper. Roast in the oven for 20 minutes, then remove the paper and continue cooking for a further 25 to 30 minutes, until the poussins are golden brown and the potatoes are tender.

SERVES 2

Celebration Turkey Mayonnaise

One of the best ways I know of serving turkey leftovers. This is an ideal dish for a party, because it is best made the day before with just the grapes and almonds added at the last minute. It goes well with most salads and is a good way of using up turkey legs after the roast.

PREPARATION AND COOKING TIME: 15 minutes
CHILLING TIME: overnight

good knob of butter
1 small onion, chopped
½ clove garlic
1 tablespoon tomato purée
½ level teaspoon curry powder
2 tablespoons lemon juice
2 tablespoons apricot jam
½ pint mayonnaise (page 152)
about 1 lb (450 g) cooked turkey, chopped
8 oz (225 g) mixed green and black grapes, halved and stoned
1½ oz (40 g) flaked almonds, toasted
small sprigs of watercress or parsley to garnish

Melt the butter in a pan, add the garlic and onion, and cook until onion is soft. Add the tomato purée, curry powder, 1 tablespoon of the lemon juice and the apricot jam, and bring to the boil, slowly stirring all the time. Purée the mixture in a blender. Transfer to a bowl, add the mayonnaise and turkey, and chill overnight in the refrigerator.

Toss the grapes in the remaining lemon juice and stir into the turkey mayonnaise. Taste and check seasoning. Pile into a serving dish and sprinkle with the flaked almonds. Garnish the dish with watercress or parsley.

SERVES 6 to 8

Glorious Turkey

This boned, gammon-stuffed bird makes a spectacular centrepiece for a cold buffet supper. Only the carcass is boned out, leaving the legs and wings to keep the shape of the bird. Cook the bacon joint a day ahead and let it cool overnight.

PREPARATION AND COOKING TIME: 5 hours
COOLING AND CHILLING TIME: overnight

2½ lb (1.2 kg) gammon joint
8 to 10 lb (3.5 to 4.5 kg) oven-ready turkey
salt
freshly ground black pepper
a little butter

STUFFING
1 lb (450 g) pork sausagemeat
2 oz (50 g) fresh brown breadcrumbs
2 heaped tablespoons chopped parsley
1 level teaspoon snipped thyme
grated rind of 1 lemon
salt
freshly ground black pepper

First cook the bacon. Put it in a pan just large enough to take the joint and cover with water. Bring to the boil, cover and simmer for 20 minutes to the pound (450 g) plus 20 minutes over – about 1¼ hours. Cool in the cooking liquid, then remove excess fat from the joint.

Remove the giblets from the turkey and untruss the bird, if necessary, so that the legs and wings are free. Put the bird on a chopping board, breast side down, and with a very sharp knife cut through the skin from tail to neck straight along the backbone to free the skin from the carcass.

Cut closely to the rib cage all the way round the bird, starting by scooping out the oyster (the fleshy part of each side of the backbone). Leave the last bone of the wing closest to the rib cage attached to the rib cage. Snap the ball and socket joint of the wing and the thigh joint close to the rib cage.

Make long, sharp cuts close to the bone, and go very carefully and slowly when near the breast bone, taking care not to poke the point of the knife through the skin. When almost at the end of the breast bone, stop and reverse the turkey. Do the other side in exactly the same way. When the tip of the breast bone is reached, slip the knife between the breast bone and skin and lift out the whole carcass.

Mix the stuffing ingredients together, seasoning well. Put the boned turkey flat, skin side down, on a board and season well. Put the stuffing on the top and round the sides of the bacon joint, bringing it up to a peak at the top, and place in a large roasting tin. Lay the turkey over the bacon and wrap the skin underneath, tucking the wing tips under at the front and securing with fine skewers or thin string. Spread with a little butter.

Roast as instructed on the turkey bag or on the chart on page 234. If the meat is browning too much, cover loosely with a piece of foil. Allow to become cold, then chill in the refrigerator before serving.

Carve straight slices across the bird, so that each slice has bacon, stuffing and turkey. Carve a little of the leg with each serving.

SERVES 16 to 20

Ballotine of Duck

Ducks do not produce a great abundance of meat. This is an excellent way of preparing a duck to serve cold for a buffet as everyone is sure to have a good slice of meat. Remove the legs and wings just before you carve as this makes for easier slicing.

PREPARATION AND COOKING TIME: 2½ hours
CHILLING TIME: overnight

1 duck, weighing about 4½ lb (2 kg)
1 oz (25 g) butter
1 tablespoon sunflower oil
1 medium-sized onion, chopped
8 oz (225 g) pork sausagemeat
8 oz (225 g) minced pork
4 chicken breasts, skinned, boned and cut into strips
2 tablespoons freshly chopped parsley
½ teaspoon ground mace
salt
freshly ground black pepper
6 quail's eggs, hard-boiled for 3 minutes and shelled
watercress and slices of orange to garnish

Start by boning the duck. Lay the duck breast side down and with a very sharp small knife cut a slit down the back of the duck. Carefully pull the skin and flesh away from the carcass by scraping the knife along the carcass in short sharp strokes to release the flesh. Continue all around the rib cage, releasing the leg and wing joints so that the whole of the rib cage can be lifted out of the duck. Leave the legs and wings in place as these will give the duck a better shape when cooked.

To make the stuffing, heat the butter and oil in a pan and fry the onion for about 5 minutes, until golden brown. Measure the sausagemeat, pork, chicken, parsley and mace into a large mixing bowl and add the fried onion.

Season lightly and mix well until thoroughly blended.

Open out the duck and season well with salt and pepper. Spread half the stuffing over the duck, then arrange the eggs end to end in a row, down the middle, and place the remaining stuffing on top. Wrap the sides of the duck up over the stuffing so that it comes back to its original 'bird' shape. Secure with skewers.

Stand the duck on a wire rack in a roasting tin and roast in the oven at 350°F/180°C/Gas Mark 4 for 2 hours, until tender. To test when the duck is cooked, pierce the thickest part of the thigh with a fine skewer: if clear juices run out, it is cooked.

Allow the duck to cool then remove the skewers, wrap in foil and chill in the refrigerator overnight before serving carved in slices. Garnish with plenty of watercress and slices of orange.

SERVES 6

Roast Duck with Cherry Sauce

Duck is so delicious, but there is not much meat. For a special occasion, serve half a duck per person. The cooking time is a very personal thing – if you like the meat to be a bit pink, cook for just 20 minutes per pound (450 g). But do make sure the duck still has a crispy skin.

PREPARATION AND COOKING TIME: 2 hours

3 ducks, weighing about 3½ lb (1.6 kg) each
salt
watercress to garnish

SAUCE
2 level teaspoons arrowroot
14 oz (397 g) can stoned black cherries, with juice reserved
4 tablespoons inexpensive port
juice of ½ orange
salt
freshly ground black pepper
cooking juices from the ducks, skimmed of fat
dash of gravy browning

Heat the oven to 375°F/190°C/Gas Mark 5. Remove the giblets from the birds, rub a little salt into the skin and stand the ducks, breast side up, on a wire rack in a roasting tin. Open roast in the oven, allowing 30 minutes per pound (450 g) for each duck, until the ducks are tender and the skin is golden brown and crisp. If necessary, turn the oven temperature up at the very end of cooking to crisp the skin.

For the sauce, measure the arrowroot into a pan, gradually blend in the juice from the cherries and bring to the boil, stirring until thickened. Stir in the cherries, port, orange juice, seasoning and the skimmed juices from the roasting tin. Taste and check the seasoning, and add a little gravy browning to give the sauce a rich colour.

To serve the ducks, take a sharp pair of kitchen scissors. Turn each duck over on its breast, snip down either side of the backbone, lift away from the bird and discard. Snip through the breast to divide the bird in two. Arrange on a large heated platter, garnished with a little sauce and watercress. Serve the rest of the sauce separately.

SERVES 6

Eighteenth-Century Pigeons

When I was researching for a good pigeon recipe, I found no less than 18 of them in my eighteenth-century book *The Art of Cooking Made Plain and Easy*. In those days pigeons were plentiful and extremely popular. Most of the recipes start off by stuffing the 'belly' with fresh sweet herbs, then slow-roasting or casseroling them. The cooking time given here may seem long for such small birds, but very often they do take three hours or even longer.

PREPARATION AND COOKING TIME: 3 hours

4 pigeons, plucked and prepared
4 sprigs fresh thyme
4 sprigs fresh parsley
4 sprigs fresh marjoram
1 tablespoon sunflower oil
large knob of butter
4 onions, sliced
4 oz (100 g) button mushrooms

1 heaped teaspoon flour
½ pint (300 ml) cider
2 chicken stock cubes, crumbled
salt
freshly ground black pepper
a little ground mace or nutmeg
chopped fresh parsley and thyme

Heat the oven to 325°F/160°C/Gas Mark 3. First take the pigeons and put a bunch of the three herbs inside each carcass. In a frying pan, heat the oil and butter until the butter has melted. Brown the birds on all sides, lift out and put to one side.

Add the onions to the pan and toss in the fat to take up all the sediment, then add the mushrooms and cook for about a minute, turning. Stir in the flour, blend well, then add the cider and stock cubes. Bring to the boil and season with salt, pepper and mace or nutmeg. Pour the mixture into a casserole large enough to take the four pigeons.

Arrange the pigeons on top of the sauce, and season the breast of the pigeons with salt and pepper. Cover and cook for 2 to 3 hours until the birds are tender (this will depend on the age of the pigeons). Check the seasoning of the onion sauce mixture and sprinkle the birds with chopped parsley and thyme before serving.

SERVES 4

Normandy Pheasant

I chose to have this very favourite recipe for a family dinner for Thomas's twentieth birthday, when I wanted something special that I could prepare ahead and just reheat in the evening. It would freeze well, too, without the cream and Calvados. With older birds cooking can take much longer. After an hour, lift the birds out of the sauce and if the legs and drumsticks are still tough, carve them off the carcass. Wrap the carcass and breast in foil to keep them moist. Return the joints to the sauce, bring to the boil and return to the oven until tender.

PREPARATION AND COOKING TIME: 1½ hours

1 oz (25 g) butter
1 tablespoon sunflower oil
brace of ovenready pheasants
1 large onion, chopped
good 1 oz (25 g) flour
¾ pint (450 ml) dry cider or white wine
1 chicken stock cube
1 tablespoon redcurrant jelly
1 large Bramley apple, peeled, cored and chopped
salt
freshly ground black pepper
2 tablespoons Calvados or brandy
6 tablespoons double cream
2 Cox's apples, cored, sliced and fried in butter to garnish

Heat the oven to 325°F/160°C/Gas Mark 3. Measure the butter and oil into a large pan. Fry the pheasants on all sides until brown, then lift out into a deep casserole just large enough to take them. Fry the onion in the fat left in the pan until golden. Add the flour, mix well and gradually blend in the cider or wine, stirring until thickened. Add the stock cube, redcurrant jelly, chopped apple and seasoning. Pour the sauce over the pheasants, cover and cook in the oven for about an hour. (Younger birds will be tender in this time; for older birds, see note above.)

Lift the pheasants out of the casserole. When cool enough to handle, joint them (I usually slice each breast diagonally in two and divide the thigh joint from the drumstick – then each person gets some of the dark leg or thigh and a piece of white breast), or if you prefer, take the meat entirely off the bones and cut into large manageable pieces.

Skim off any fat from the sauce, then bring the sauce to the boil. Check seasoning, draw to one side of the heat, add the cream and Calvados or brandy and pour over the meat. Garnish with fried apple slices.

SERVES 6 to 8

Jugged Hare

A traditional winter casserole. Serve with forcemeat balls and a fruit jelly. The gravy is thickened with beurre manié – just equal quantities of butter and flour, creamed together and then dropped into the hot gravy.

PREPARATION AND COOKING TIME: 5½ hours
MARINATING TIME: overnight

1 hare, jointed
2 oz (50 g) streaky bacon, cut in strips
3 oz (75 g) butter
2 onions, chopped
2 tablespoons redcurrant jelly
¼ pint (150 ml) inexpensive port
grated rind and juice of ½ lemon
4 sticks celery, chopped
salt
2 oz (50 g) flour

MARINADE
½ pint (300 ml) red wine
2 bay leaves
freshly ground black pepper
2 cloves garlic, quartered
2 tablespoons sunflower oil
1 onion, sliced

FORCEMEAT BALLS
2 oz (50 g) cooked bacon, snipped
2 oz (50 g) shredded suet
grated rind of 1 lemon
2 tablespoons chopped parsley
4 oz (100 g) white breadcrumbs
1 egg, beaten
a little butter and oil for frying

Combine all the ingredients for the marinade. Put two large strong freezer bags one inside the other and put the jointed hare and marinade into the bag. Seal and leave overnight in the refrigerator.

Heat the oven to 325°F/160°C/Gas Mark 3. Remove hare from the marinade, then strain liquid and set to one side. Fry the streaky bacon gently for 2 minutes, add 1 oz (25 g) of the butter and fry the hare joints a few at a time until browned. Transfer to a fireproof casserole dish. Add the onion to the pan and fry until softened. Add the redcurrant jelly and stir until dissolved, then pour over the hare with the port, lemon rind and juice, celery and seasoning. Make the reserved marinade up to 1 pint (600 ml) with water and add to the casserole. Bring to the boil, cover and simmer for 5 minutes, then transfer to the oven and cook until tender – 4 to 6 hours, according to how old the hare is.

Cream the remaining butter with the flour. Lift the hare joints out of the casserole with a slotted spoon and add teaspoons of the beurre manié to the hot liquid. Bring to the boil and stir until thickened, then return the hare to the casserole and check seasoning.

Meanwhile, prepare the forcemeat balls. Blend all the ingredients except the butter and oil together and season well. Roll into about twelve balls, then fry in the butter and oil until crisp and brown on all sides. Add to the jugged hare just before serving.

SERVES 6

Rabbit in Mustard Sauce

It is difficult to be accurate with the suggested cooking time as this will depend on the age of the rabbit, so keep testing by prodding the thickest part of a joint with a skewer – the meat should not fall off the bone. Serve with a colourful vegetable.

PREPARATION AND COOKING TIME: 1¼ hours

1 rabbit, jointed
½ pint (300 ml) good chicken stock
1 large onion, chopped
1 bay leaf
thinly peeled rind of 1 lemon
salt
freshly ground black pepper
croûtons of fried bread to garnish (page 103)

SAUCE
about ½ pint (300 ml) milk
1 oz (25 g) butter
1 oz (25 g) flour
1 scant level tablespoon dry mustard
1 scant tablespoon sugar
1 tablespoon vinegar

Heat the oven to 350°F/180°C/Gas Mark 4. Put the rabbit, stock, onion, bay leaf, lemon zest and seasoning in a casserole. Cover and cook in the oven for about an hour, or until tender. Transfer the rabbit to a plate, using a slotted spoon.

Discard the bay leaf, then make the stock up to ¾ pint (450 ml) with milk. Make a roux by melting the butter in a large saucepan and adding the flour. Cook for a minute, without colouring, then stir in the milk and stock and bring to the boil, stirring until thickened. Blend the mustard, sugar and vinegar together and add to the sauce. Taste and check seasoning.

Place the rabbit in the sauce and heat through, then transfer to a serving dish. Garnish with croûtons of fried bread.

SERVES 4

Highland Venison

If you are lucky enough to find some venison, this is a deliciously tender dish. Also very good made into a pie: cool the mixture, put into a 2½ pint (1.4 litre) pie dish, cover with puff pastry and bake in a hot oven (425°F/220°C/ Gas Mark 7) for about 30 minutes.

PREPARATION AND COOKING TIME: 3 hours
MARINATING TIME: overnight

1½ lb (675 g) stewing venison
4 oz (100 g) fatty bacon, cubed
3 oz (75 g) piece German smoked
  sausage, skinned and sliced
1 large onion, chopped
1½ oz (40 g) flour
about ½ pint (300 ml) good beef
  stock
bouquet garni
1 tablespoon bramble jelly
salt
freshly ground black pepper
dash of gravy browning

MARINADE
½ pint (300 ml) red wine
2 bay leaves
8 peppercorns
2 cloves garlic, quartered
1 onion, sliced
2 tablespoons sunflower oil

Cut the venison into ¾ inch (2 cm) cubes. Combined all the marinade ingredients, add the venison and leave to marinate for 24 hours in the refrigerator.

Lift the meat out of the marinade. Strain the marinade and set to one side, and discard the bay leaves, peppercorns, garlic and onion.

Put the bacon into a non-stick frying pan and cook slowly to draw out the fat. Add the sliced sausage and onion, and cook for about 10 minutes, until the bacon is crispy. Add the flour and blend well. Make the reserved marinade up to 1 pint (600 ml) with stock, stir into the pan and bring to the boil, stirring. Add the venison, bouquet garni and bramble jelly. Season well, add the gravy browning and return to the boil.

Transfer to a casserole, cover and cook in the oven at 325°F/160°C/Gas Mark 3 for about 2½ hours, or until the venison is tender. (Remember to remove the bouquet garni before serving.)

SERVES 6

PASTA, RICE AND QUICHES

A wonderful choice of pasta is available – my favourite varieties are penne, 'shells' (especially with fish) and tagliatelle. Pasta is quick to cook as a side dish and forms the basis of many main-dish favourites too.

Brown rice is gaining in popularity, and my family prefer it when it is not cooked for quite so long as recommended on the packet. That way, it retains a nice nuttiness.

There can be few things worse than a quiche with a soggy base. It really is worth baking quiches blind so that the base remains crisp and delicious.

Penne Napoletana

Such a simple pasta dish, but so good. If you prefer, use other small pasta shapes instead of penne.

PREPARATION AND COOKING TIME: 1 hour

8 oz (225 g) calabrese or broccoli
6 oz (175 g) penne
1 large onion, chopped
2 fat cloves garlic, crushed
1 tablespoon oil
knob of butter
4 oz (100 g) button mushrooms,
    sliced
1 red pepper, seeded and sliced
8 oz (225 g) courgettes, sliced
3 oz (75 g) well-flavoured Cheddar
    cheese, grated

SAUCE
2 oz (50 g) butter
2 oz (50 g) flour
1 pint (600 ml) milk
1 teaspoon Dijon mustard
salt
freshly ground black pepper
freshly grated nutmeg
1 egg, beaten

Slice all the stalk from the calabrese, boil them in salted water for 5 minutes, then add the broken up heads and cook for a further 3 minutes. Drain in a colander and refresh under running cold water. Cook the pasta in plenty of boiling water as directed on the packet until al dente, then drain and rinse under running cold water.

In a large frying pan, fry the onion and garlic in the oil and butter until tender. Add the mushrooms, pepper and courgettes and fry quickly for about 3 minutes. Remove from the heat, stir in the calabrese and season well.

Heat the butter for the sauce, add the flour, cook for a minute, then gradually blend in the milk. Bring to the boil, stirring until thickened. Season with the mustard, nutmeg, salt and pepper. Remove from the heat, stir in the egg, vegetables and pasta, and turn into a large shallow ovenproof dish. Scatter the cheese over the top.

Cook in the oven at 400°F/200°C/Gas Mark 6 for about 45 minutes, until golden brown.

SERVES 6

Spaghetti Carbonara

This is the sort of supper dish that can be served after a trip to the cinema or theatre. All the ingredients can be prepared ahead, the garlic and bacon fried, the tagliatelle weighed out and the eggs beaten with the cheese – then the dish just needs assembling when you come back in. Really quick and easy to prepare, and delicious served with a crisp green salad.

PREPARATION AND COOKING TIME: 30 minutes

6 oz (175 g) streaky bacon
1 fat clove garlic, crushed
1 lb (450 g) spaghetti
6 eggs
4 oz (100 g) Parmesan cheese, grated
salt
freshly ground black pepper
¼ pint (150 ml) single cream

Cook the bacon in a non-stick pan over a gentle heat until the fat begins to run out, then increase the heat. Add the garlic and fry quickly until the bacon is crisp. Meanwhile, cook the spaghetti in a large pan of boiling salted water as directed on the packet. Break the eggs into a bowl, add the cheese and plenty of seasoning, and beat well until blended.

When the spaghetti is cooked, drain thoroughly and return to the hot pan. Add the bacon and the egg mixture, and cook over a moderate heat, stirring continuously, until the egg is lightly set. Stir in the cream and continue to cook until heated through, then serve straightaway.

SERVES 6

Tomato Baked Noodles

This recipe will serve 6 to 8 instead of a potato dish with cold meat salads. For convenience, you can prepare it all well ahead and then just reheat as below.

PREPARATION AND COOKING TIME: 1 hour

½ oz (15 g) butter
1 tablespoon sunflower oil
1 large onion, chopped
14 oz (397 g) can chopped tomatoes
3 tablespoons tomato purée
1 teaspoon sugar
salt
freshly ground black pepper
8 oz (225 g) tagliatelle
8 oz (225 g) well-flavoured Cheddar cheese, thinly sliced
1½ oz (40 g) Parmesan cheese, grated

Heat the butter and oil in a large pan and quickly fry the onion until soft and beginning to brown. Stir in the tomatoes, tomato purée, sugar, salt and pepper. Bring to the boil and simmer gently for about 15 minutes, until thick and pulpy. Taste and check seasoning.

Cook the pasta in a pan of boiling salted water as directed on the packet until just tender. Drain and rinse under running hot water.

To assemble the dish, arrange the pasta, tomato sauce and cheese in layers in a lightly buttered, large ovenproof dish, finishing with a layer of cheese. Cook in the oven at 375°F/190°C/Gas Mark 5 for about 45 minutes, until the sauce is bubbling and the cheese is golden brown.

SERVES 4

Pasta Marinière

This brings back wonderful memories of eating out of doors in southern Italy. Serve in soup bowls with spoons so that none of the sauce is wasted. If you are using the tiny queen scallops, leave them whole.

PREPARATION AND COOKING TIME: 15 minutes

8 oz (225 g) large pasta shells
2 tablespoons good olive oil
4 shallots, chopped finely
1 fat clove garlic, crushed
4 oz (100 g) squid, cut into strips or rings
4 oz (100 g) shelled mussels
4 oz (100 g) scallops, halved
4 oz (100 g) peeled prawns
4 fl oz (120 ml) white wine
¼ pint (150 ml) double cream
4 tablespoons freshly chopped parsley
salt
freshly ground black pepper

Cook the pasta in plenty of boiling salted water until al dente, then drain and set to one side.

Heat 1 tablespoon of the oil and cook the shallots and garlic for about 2 minutes. Add the squid and cook for 3 minutes, then add the mussels and scallops and cook for a further 2 minutes, stirring well. Lastly, add the prawns and white wine, cook for a minute then add the cream and chopped parsley (saving a little to sprinkle over the finished dish). Bring to the boil and stir in the pasta and seasoning. Serve immediately, sprinkled with the remaining parsley.

SERVES 4

Tuna Tagliatelle

I fall back on this recipe time and time again when the fridge is bare. I've always a can of tuna, pasta, eggs, milk and cheese in the house. If time is short I forget the breadcrumb topping and use cheese alone.

PREPARATION AND COOKING TIME: 1 hour

8 oz (225 g) tagliatelle
1 onion, finely sliced
3½ oz (85 g) butter
2 oz (50 g) flour
1 pint (600 ml) milk
7 oz (200 g) can tuna in oil, drained
3 hard-boiled eggs, coarsely chopped
salt
freshly ground black pepper
4 oz (100 g) mature Cheddar cheese, grated
3 oz (75 g) wholemeal breadcrumbs

Boil the tagliatelle and onion together in a pan of salted water for about 12 minutes, until the pasta is al dente. Drain well and set to one side. Melt 2 oz (50 g) of the butter in a pan, add the flour and cook for a minute, then gradually add the milk and bring to the boil, stirring until thickened. Stir in the tuna, eggs, seasoning and cheese, and turn into a 3½ pint (2 litre) shallow ovenproof dish. Fry the breadcrumbs in the remaining butter until crisp, then sprinkle over the tagliatelle.

Cook in the oven at 400°F/200°C/Gas Mark 6 for about 45 minutes, until hot through and browned on top.

SERVES 6

Lasagne

An Italian classic, and a marvellous dish for the freezer.

PREPARATION AND COOKING TIME: 1¼ hours

6 oz (175 g) Barilla or other 'no-
  precook' lasagne
2 oz (50 g) Cheddar cheese, grated
1 oz (25 g) Parmesan cheese,
  grated
2 oz (50 g) Gruyère cheese, grated

WHITE SAUCE
2 oz (50 g) butter
1½ oz (40 g) flour
1 pint (600 ml) milk
1 teaspoon Dijon mustard
a little grated nutmeg
salt
freshly ground black pepper

MEAT SAUCE
2 oz (50 g) bacon, chopped
2 lb (900 g) lean minced beef
1½ oz (40 g) flour
6 sticks celery, chopped
12 oz (350 g) onion, chopped
½ pint (300 ml) good beef stock
2 fat cloves garlic, crushed
14 oz (397 g) can chopped tomatoes
4 good tablespoons tomato purée
1 teaspoon sugar
1 teaspoon fresh thyme, chopped
salt
freshly ground black pepper

First prepare the meat sauce. Put the bacon in a non-stick pan and fry gently until the fat begins to run, then add the mince. Increase heat and fry quickly until browned, then add the flour and blend well. Stir in all the remaining ingredients, bring to the boil and cover with a lid. Simmer for about an hour, until the meat is tender.

Meanwhile, make the white sauce. Melt the butter in a pan, add the flour and cook for a minute, then gradually add the milk and bring to the boil, stirring until thickened. Remove from heat and stir in the mustard, nutmeg and seasoning.

In a 9 by 12 inch (23 by 30 cm) shallow ovenproof dish, put layers of meat sauce, lasagne, white sauce then cheese. Repeat the layers, finishing with cheese on top. Do not overlap the lasagne – if necessary, break the pieces to fit into the dish.

Cook uncovered at 375°F/190°C/Gas Mark 5 for 45 to 60 minutes, until heated through and crispy brown on top.

SERVES 6

Rice and Prawn Salad

Do not use dried mint instead of fresh as it does not work nearly as well. Use a few freshly snipped chives instead, if you have them.

PREPARATION AND COOKING TIME: 25 minutes
CHILLING TIME: 3 hours

8 oz (225 g) long-grain rice
1 large red pepper, seeded and chopped
3 spring onions, finely sliced
8 oz (225 g) shelled prawns
1 teaspoon paprika
1 teaspoon dry mustard
salt
freshly ground black pepper
2 teaspoons caster sugar
2 tablespoons freshly chopped mint
5 tablespoons sunflower oil
2 tablespoons white wine vinegar
juice of 1 small orange
a few drops of Tabasco sauce

Cook the rice in boiling salted water until just tender. Drain and rinse under warm running water, then drain again thoroughly. Turn the rice into a large bowl and stir in the chopped pepper, spring onions and prawns. In another bowl, blend together all the remaining ingredients then pour over the rice mixture and mix well.

Cover with clingfilm and chill in the refrigerator for about 3 hours. Taste to check seasoning, then transfer to a clean serving bowl.

SERVES 4 to 6

Portuguese Rice

The rice I used was Uncle Ben's wholegrain and it cooked in 20 minutes – do not be tempted to overcook.

PREPARATION AND COOKING TIME: 30 minutes

a little olive oil
6 rashers streaky bacon, cut into thin strips
3/4 pint (450 ml) boiling water
3 oz (75 g) onion, chopped
6 oz (175 g) wholegrain rice
1 chicken stock cube
1 oz (25 g) raisins
2 tablespoons soy sauce
freshly ground black pepper
salt

Measure the oil into a pan, add the bacon and heat until just beginning to sizzle. Cook for a few moments, then add the water, onion, rice and stock cube. Stir well, bring to the boil, cover and simmer for about 20 minutes, until the rice is cooked but still firm.

Drain off any excess liquid and add the raisins, soy sauce and pepper to taste. A little salt may be necessary too. Serve hot.

SERVES 2 or 3

RIGHT: *Penne Napoletana (page 121)*

Mushroom Koulibiac

This dish is ideal to serve if you have invited vegetarian friends for a meal – but all your other guests will enjoy it too! Serve with thick Greek yoghurt instead of soured cream, if you prefer.

PREPARATION AND COOKING TIME: 1¼ hours

4 oz (100 g) brown long-grain rice
1 oz (25 g) butter
1 scant tablespoon sunflower oil
1 onion, chopped
8 oz (225 g) mushrooms, sliced
½ small white cabbage, shredded
3 hard-boiled eggs, roughly chopped
salt
freshly ground black pepper

2 tablespoons freshly chopped
  parsley
14 oz (400 g) packet frozen puff
  pastry, thawed
1 egg, beaten
2 oz (50 g) butter, melted
juice of ½ lemon
¼ pint (150 ml) soured cream

Cook the rice in a pan of boiling salted water, following the packet directions, then drain and rinse well. Heat the butter and oil in a pan and sauté the onion until soft, then add the mushrooms and cook until they are just beginning to soften. Blanch the shredded cabbage in a pan of boiling salted water for a minute then drain well. Carefully combine the rice, onion, mushrooms, cabbage, eggs, seasoning and parsley together in a bowl.

Roll out the pastry to a rectangle about 11 by 16 inches (27.5 by 40 cm), trimming off a little to use for decoration. Pile the rice mixture down the centre of the pastry, leaving a wide border of pastry round the edges. Brush the border with beaten egg, then fold over both long sides so that they overlap, making a fat sausage shape. Tuck the ends under the roll. Lift the roll on to a baking sheet, and score across the top three or four times with a knife. Roll out the pastry trimmings and use to make a lattice over the top of the koulibiac. Brush all over with beaten egg. Bake in the oven at 400°F/200°C/Gas Mark 6 for about 40 minutes, until golden brown.

Using two fish slices, carefully transfer the koulibiac to a serving dish and pour the melted butter and lemon juice down the scored cuts. Serve with a bowl of soured cream.

SERVES 6

LEFT: *Green Salad with Fennel (page 146), Rice and Prawn Salad (page 127) and Tomato and Avocado Salad (page 144)*

Stuffed Green Peppers

A good supper dish to serve in the summer when peppers are at their cheapest. Do remember that brown rice takes longer to cook than white rice. I like to accompany this with warm, crisp French bread.

PREPARATION AND COOKING TIME: 1¾ hours

6 large green peppers
6 oz (175 g) brown long-grain rice
1½ oz (40 g) butter
1 medium-sized onion, chopped
6 oz (175 g) button mushrooms,
   sliced
4 oz (100 g) back bacon, chopped
4 oz (100 g) chicken livers, chopped
salt
freshly ground black pepper
2 tablespoons freshly chopped
   parsley
2 eggs, beaten

CHEESE SAUCE
2 oz (50 g) butter
2 oz (50 g) flour
1 pint (600 ml) milk
1 teaspoon made mustard
grated nutmeg
salt
freshly ground black pepper
8 oz (225 g) well-flavoured
   Cheddar cheese, grated

Cut a circle from the top of each of the peppers to remove the stem and seeds. Arrange the peppers in a shallow ovenproof dish so that they are just touching.

Cook the rice in a pan of boiling salted water as directed on the packet, then drain and rinse well. Melt the butter in a large pan and fry the onion, mushrooms, bacon and chicken livers for about 10 minutes, until the onion has softened. Stir in the cooked rice, salt, pepper and parsley. Remove from the heat and stir in the eggs to bind the rice together. Divide this filling between the peppers.

For the cheese sauce, melt the butter in a large pan, stir in the flour and cook for a minute. Gradually blend in the milk and bring to the boil, stirring until thickened. Remove from the heat and stir in the mustard, a little nutmeg, salt, pepper and about a quarter of the cheese. Mix well and pour the sauce over and around the peppers. Sprinkle with the remaining cheese and bake in the oven at 350°F/180°C/Gas Mark 4 for about an hour, until the peppers are tender.

SERVES 6

Nasi Goreng

This dish was brought to Holland from Indonesia when the Dutch ruled there. It is still very popular today. This version is inexpensive and we have enjoyed it for umpteen years.

PREPARATION AND COOKING TIME: 45 minutes

1 lb (450 g) boned shoulder of pork
4 tablespoons sunflower oil
8 oz (225 g) onions, sliced
8 oz (225 g) long-grain rice
8 oz (225 g) packet frozen mixed
  vegetables
4 tablespoons soy sauce
1 level teaspoon curry powder
salt
freshly ground black pepper
4 tomatoes, cut into wedges, to
  garnish

OMELETTE
1 egg
1 teaspoon cold water
salt
freshly ground black pepper
knob of butter

Cut the pork into ½ inch (1.25 cm) cubes. Heat the oil in a large pan, add the pork and onions and fry quickly for 5 minutes. Reduce the heat, cover the pan and cook gently for 30 minutes, stirring occasionally.

Meanwhile, cook the rice in boiling salted water for about 12 minutes, or as directed on the packet, then drain well and rinse in warm water. Cook the vegetables as directed on the packet and drain well.

Stir the soy sauce, curry powder and seasoning into the pork with the rice and vegetables, and mix thoroughly. Check seasoning and heat gently.

To prepare the omelette, mix the egg and water together with seasoning to taste. Melt the butter in a small pan and pour in the egg mixture. Cook gently, undisturbed, until the underside is golden brown, then turn over and lightly brown the second side. Slip the omelette on to a plate and cut into strips.

Pile the rice on a serving dish and arrange the omelette strips on top in a lattice. Garnish with tomato wedges.

SERVES 4 to 6

Quiche Lorraine

A really large quiche for a crowd, delicious served warm with salad. If you prefer, halve the ingredients and cook in a 7 to 8 inch (18 to 20 cm) flan tin. (A smaller quiche will need a slightly shorter cooking time.)

PREPARATION AND COOKING TIME: 1 hour
CHILLING TIME: 30 minutes

1 oz (25 g) butter
1 tablespoon sunflower oil
1 large onion, chopped
12 oz (350 g) streaky bacon,
  snipped into small pieces
8 oz (225 g) well-flavoured
  Cheddar cheese, grated
4 eggs, beaten
1/2 pint (300 ml) milk

1/4 pint (150 ml) single cream
salt
freshly ground black pepper
freshly chopped parsley

PASTRY
8 oz (225 g) plain flour
4 oz (100 g) butter or margarine
about 3 tablespoons water

For the pastry, put the flour in a bowl and rub in the fats until the mixture resembles fine breadcrumbs. Add the water and bind together to form a firm dough. Knead until smooth then roll out on a lightly floured surface and use to line a deep 11 inch (27.5 cm) loose-bottomed flan tin. Chill in the refrigerator for about 30 minutes.

Place a thick baking sheet in the oven, then heat the oven to 425°F/220°C/Gas Mark 7. Standing the quiche on a hot baking sheet to cook will ensure that the bottom browns nicely. Line the flan case with greaseproof paper and baking beans, or a piece of foil, and bake in the oven for about 20 minutes; remove the paper and beans or foil for the last 10 minutes.

Meanwhile, heat the butter and oil in a pan and fry the onion and bacon for about 10 minutes, until the onion is golden brown and the bacon crisp. Spoon over the base of the flan case and sprinkle the cheese on top. In a large jug, mix the eggs, milk, cream, seasoning and parsley until thoroughly blended, then pour into the flan case.

Reduce the oven temperature to 350°F/180°C/Gas Mark 4. Place the quiche in the oven and cook for about 35 minutes, until the filling has set.

SERVES 8

Cheese and Spinach Quiche

To get a brown base to the quiche, bake on a thick metal baking sheet that has been preheated in the oven.

PREPARATION AND COOKING TIME: 1 hour
CHILLING TIME: 20 minutes

8 oz (225 g) packet frozen leaf spinach, thawed and drained
1/4 pint (150 ml) natural yoghurt
1/4 pint (150 ml) soured cream
salt
freshly ground black pepper
2 eggs
2 oz (50 g) Cheddar cheese, grated

PASTRY
6 oz (175 g) plain flour
3 oz (75 g) margarine
1 1/2 oz (40 g) Parmesan cheese, grated
1 egg yolk
about 1 1/2 tablespoons water

Heat the oven to 425°F/220°C/Gas Mark 7, and heat a baking sheet in the oven. Put the flour for the pastry in a bowl and rub in the margarine until the mixture resembles fine breadcrumbs. Stir in the Parmesan cheese. Mix the egg yolk with the water and stir into the flour to give a firm dough. Roll out on a lightly floured surface and use to line a 9 inch (22.5 cm) loose-bottomed flan tin. Chill in the refrigerator for 20 minutes.

Bake the flan case blind, using a round piece of greaseproof paper and baking beans or a piece of foil, for 20 minutes, removing the paper and beans or foil for the last 10 minutes.

Spread the spinach over the base of the flan. In a bowl, mix together the yoghurt, cream, salt, pepper and eggs, then pour over the spinach and sprinkle with the cheese. Reduce the oven temperature to 350°F/180°C/Gas Mark 4 and bake the quiche for about 20 minutes, until the filling is set and a pale golden brown.

SERVES 4

VEGETABLES AND SALADS

Some vegetables are best just cooked simply. You can spin out expensive vegetables such as mange-tout by combining them with a cheaper vegetable, or transform a simple salad by adding just a few leaves of something colourful such as radicchio.

Buy vegetables very much in season. They will then have more flavour and be far less expensive. Look in the market for whatever is fresh and plentiful – you can swap vegetables successfully in many recipes according to what you have available.

If you are making a leafy salad using French dressing, don't toss it until just before serving. Chunky salads in mayonnaise, on the other hand, benefit from long marinating in a cool place.

Garden Vegetables au Gratin

This really is a very versatile dish, and I tend to use whatever vegetables I have available from the garden or those which seem the best buy in the shops. Another good combination is courgettes, cauliflower sprigs and red or green peppers.

PREPARATION AND COOKING TIME: 1 hour

1 tablespoon sunflower oil
1 oz (25 g) butter
1 large onion, chopped
1 fat clove garlic, crushed
1 lb (450 g) young carrots, sliced
1 lb (450 g) courgettes, sliced
salt
freshly ground black pepper
1 lb (450 g) tomatoes, skinned
  (page 17) and sliced

TOPPING
1½ oz (40 g) butter
1½ oz (40 g) flour
¾ pint (450 ml) milk
salt
freshly ground black pepper
1 teaspoon Dijon mustard
½ teaspoon grated nutmeg
1 egg, beaten
3 oz (75 g) well-flavoured Cheddar
  cheese, grated

Heat the oil and butter in a large pan, and fry the onion, garlic and carrots gently for about 10 minutes, until just beginning to soften. Increase the heat, add the courgettes and stir-fry with the onion and carrot for about 5 minutes. Season well. Turn the vegetables into a large, shallow ovenproof dish and top with the slices of tomato.

For the topping, heat the butter in a pan, add the flour and cook for a minute, then gradually blend in the milk and bring to the boil, stirring until thickened. Season well, adding the mustard and nutmeg, then remove from the heat and stir in the egg. Pour over the vegetables and sprinkle with the cheese. Either brown under a hot grill or put in the oven at 400°C/200°C/Gas Mark 6 for about 20 minutes, until the cheese has melted and is golden brown.

SERVES 6

Baked Fennel with Lemon

Choose fennel heads that are white in colour: those that are green tend to be a little bitter.

PREPARATION AND COOKING TIME: 1½ hours

4 heads of fennel
salt
freshly ground black pepper
2 oz (50 g) butter
juice of 1 large lemon
a little freshly chopped parsley

Heat the oven to 350°F/180°C/Gas Mark 4. Cut each head of fennel into about six wedges and arrange in a large shallow ovenproof dish in layers, seasoning well between each layer. Dot with the butter and pour over the lemon juice. Cover with a lid or piece of foil and bake in the oven for about 1¼ hours, until the fennel is tender.

Serve hot, sprinkled with a little freshly chopped parsley.

SERVES 6

Green Beans
with Tomato and Onion Sauce

Take care not to overcook the beans. They should still have a crunch in the middle.

PREPARATION AND COOKING TIME: 15 minutes

1½ lb (675 g) French beans
1 tablespoon sunflower oil
1 medium-sized onion, chopped
1 fat clove garlic, crushed
14 oz (397 g) can tomatoes
salt
freshly ground black pepper
1 teaspoon sugar

Trim the beans and cook in a pan of boiling salted water for about 8 minutes, until just tender, then drain well and arrange in a serving dish.

Heat the oil in a pan and fry the onion and garlic for about 5 minutes, until beginning to soften. Add the contents of the can of tomatoes and continue to cook without a lid until thick and pulpy. Stir in the salt, pepper and sugar, and pour over the beans. Serve at once.

SERVES 6

Peas and Mange-Tout

Mange-tout are expensive to buy but are so nice to serve for a party. Serving them mixed with peas stretches them a bit further and helps the cost. You could also use sliced courgettes instead of mange-tout.

PREPARATION AND COOKING TIME: 15 minutes

8 oz (225 g) mange-tout
12 oz (350 g) frozen peas or petits pois, thawed
generous knob of butter

Top and tail the mange-tout and string if necessary. Put them into a large pan of boiling salted water with the peas. Bring back to the boil, cover with a lid and simmer gently for about 3 minutes, until just tender. Drain thoroughly.

Return the peas and mange-tout to the pan and toss in butter over a gentle heat. Turn out into a warm dish to serve.

SERVES 4 to 6

New York Potatoes

I prefer to use baby new potatoes for this recipe, but when they are not available use larger potatoes cut into small pieces.

PREPARATION AND COOKING TIME: 1 hour

1½ lb (675 g) baby new potatoes, scraped
2 oz (50 g) butter
3 fat cloves garlic, peeled
salt
freshly ground black pepper
about 2 tablespoons mixed chopped fresh parsley and chives

Heat the oven to 375°F/190°C/Gas Mark 5. Dry the potatoes thoroughly. Put the butter in a large, shallow ovenproof dish and heat in the oven until melted. Add the potatoes and roll them in the butter until evenly coated, then add the garlic and season well. Cover with foil and cook in the oven for about 30 minutes, shaking the dish occasionally until the potatoes are evenly coated with butter.

Remove the foil and cook for a further 30 minutes, or until the potatoes are tender. Remove the garlic cloves. Turn the potatoes into a warm serving dish and pour over any remaining butter. Sprinkle with parsley and chives.

SERVES 4 to 6

Garlic Cheese Potatoes

These potatoes go well with plainly cooked meat such as grilled chops.

PREPARATION AND COOKING TIME: 1¾ hours

1 oz (25 g) butter
2 fat cloves garlic, peeled and crushed
1½ lb (675 g) potatoes, peeled and thinly sliced
salt
freshly ground black pepper
about 4 oz (100 g) well-flavoured Cheddar cheese, grated
¾ pint (450 ml) milk
1 egg

Preheat the oven to 375°F/190°C/Gas Mark 5. Butter an ovenproof dish generously with about half the butter, then spread the crushed garlic over the bottom and sides of the dish. Arrange the potatoes in layers in the dish, seasoning well between each layer with salt, pepper and a sprinkling of cheese.

Heat the milk until almost boiling then beat in the egg. Pour over the potatoes. Dot with butter and sprinkle with the remaining cheese, then bake in the oven for about 1½ hours, or until the potatoes are tender.

SERVES 4 to 6

Cabbage au Gratin

This recipe certainly livens up a cabbage. The dish can be prepared ahead and kept in the refrigerator until required. To serve, reheat in the oven at 350°F/180°C/Gas Mark 4 for about 30 minutes, until heated through.

PREPARATION AND COOKING TIME: 30 minutes

1 large white cabbage, shredded
2 oz (50 g) butter
2 oz (50 g) flour
1 pint (600 ml) milk
2 teaspoons Dijon mustard
salt
freshly ground black pepper
½ teaspoon grated nutmeg
6 oz (175 g) well-flavoured Cheddar cheese, grated
2 oz (50 g) fresh white breadcrumbs

Cook the cabbage in a little boiling salted water for about 10 minutes, so that it is still crisp. Drain thoroughly.

Melt the butter in a pan, stir in the flour and cook for a minute. Gradually blend in the milk and bring to the boil, stirring until thickened. Stir in the mustard, salt, pepper, nutmeg and half the cheese, and mix well. Toss the cooked cabbage in the sauce until thoroughly coated, then turn into a warmed serving dish.

Mix the remaining cheese and breadcrumbs together, and sprinkle over the cabbage. Put under a hot grill for a few moments, until the sauce is bubbling and the cheese and breadcrumbs are golden brown.

SERVES 8

Red Cabbage

Delicious served with grilled pork chops and other grills.

PREPARATION AND COOKING TIME: 50 minutes

1 small red cabbage
12 oz (350 g) cooking apples, sliced
¼ pint (150 ml) water
1½ oz (40 g) sugar
salt
3 cloves
5 tablespoons vinegar
2 oz (50 g) butter
1 tablespoon redcurrant jelly

Finely shred the cabbage and put in a pan with the apples and water. Add the sugar, salt and cloves, cover and simmer for about 45 minutes, or until tender.

Remove the cloves from the pan. Add the vinegar, butter and redcurrant jelly, and stir until the butter has melted. Taste and check seasoning.

SERVES 4 to 6

American Iceberg Salad

The salad and dressing can be made well in advance. Iceberg lettuce is wonderful in that it stays crisp much longer than other lettuces.

PREPARATION TIME: 15 minutes

1 small iceberg lettuce
1 bunch watercress
3 oz (75 g) button mushrooms, sliced
2 courgettes, sliced
½ bunch spring onions, chopped
1 small red pepper, seeded and diced

DRESSING
3 tablespoons mayonnaise (page 152)
3 tablespoons soured cream
2 tablespoons white wine vinegar
salt
freshly ground black pepper
1 fat clove garlic, crushed

Shred the lettuce and put it in a large salad bowl with the watercress, broken into small sprigs. Add the mushrooms, courgettes, spring onions and red pepper, and toss well.

For the dressing, blend all the ingredients together and serve in a small bowl along with the salad.

SERVES 6

Tomato and Avocado Salad

Make this into a main meal salad by adding sliced cold chicken and, if you like, a little chopped spring onion. If you are in a hurry there is no need to skin the tomatoes, as long as they are firm.

PREPARATION TIME: 10 minutes
CHILLING TIME: 20 minutes

1 large avocado pear
1 tablespoon lemon juice
1 lb (450 g) firm tomatoes, skinned and sliced
about 5 tablespoons French dressing (page 153)

Half an hour before serving, peel the skin from the avocado, cut in half, and remove the stone. Cut the flesh in slices and sprinkle with lemon juice to prevent discoloration.

Arrange the tomato slices on a large serving dish with the avocado slices on top, radiating outwards from the centre. Chill in the refrigerator. Spoon over the French dressing just before serving.

SERVES 4

Swiss Salad

This is a wonderfully coloured and textured salad to serve on more special occasions – all the colours of green from light to dark, with the glowing red of the radicchio. If batavia lettuce is unavailable, use another crisp lettuce such as iceberg.

PREPARATION TIME: 5 minutes

½ batavia lettuce
a few heads lamb's lettuce
1 curly endive, sliced
a few radicchio leaves
1 tablespoon freshly chopped dill
4 tablespoons French dressing (see page 153)

Break the batavia leaves into small pieces in the salad bowl. Add the lamb's lettuce, sliced curly endive, radicchio leaves and dill.

Just before serving, add the French dressing and toss well.

SERVES 6

Green Salad with Fennel

This is quite one of my favourite salads. The fennel really does lift an ordinary green salad. Don't add the dressing to the salad too soon before serving, otherwise the lettuce will begin to go limp.

PREPARATION TIME: 10 minutes
CHILLING TIME: 2 hours

1 head of fennel, thinly sliced
6 sticks of celery, chopped
6 tablespoons French dressing (page 153)
1 lettuce
½ cucumber
1 small green pepper
1 bunch of watercress

Place the fennel, celery and dressing in a bowl. Cover with clingfilm and chill in the refrigerator for about 2 hours.

To assemble the salad, wash and drain the lettuce, break into small pieces and place in a serving bowl. Slice the cucumber, cut the pepper into thin strips after discarding the seeds and pith, and wash the watercress. Add all these to the lettuce. Just before serving, add the fennel, celery and dressing and toss together. Serve straightaway.

SERVES 6

Yoghurt, Mint and Cucumber Salad

This is a good salad to serve in summer with barbecued food – very good with kebabs and steaks.

PREPARATION TIME: 5 minutes
STANDING TIME: 20 minutes

1 cucumber
salt
1 pint (600 ml) plain yoghurt
4 to 5 rounded teaspoons freshly chopped mint
freshly ground black pepper

Leaving the skin on, cut the cucumber into small dice. Put on a large plate, sprinkle with a little salt, cover with another plate and leave to stand for 20 minutes. Drain off any liquid.

Put the yoghurt in a bowl and stir in the cucumber, mint and pepper. Taste and check seasoning, then turn into a serving dish.

SERVES 6

Coleslaw

This is a fairly classic recipe, and I often add chopped celery or diced apple if I have some to hand.

PREPARATION TIME: 10 minutes
CHILLING AND STANDING TIME: overnight plus 1 hour

1 small hard white cabbage, weighing about 1½ lb (675 g)
¼ pint (150 ml) French dressing (page 153)
salt
freshly ground black pepper
1 level teaspoon Dijon mustard
1 small onion, very finely chopped
2 carrots
5 to 6 tablespoons mayonnaise (page 152)

Cut the cabbage into quarters, trim away and discard any hard stalk, then finely slice into strips. Put the cabbage in a large roomy bowl with the French dressing, seasoning, mustard and onion, and toss very well. Cover with a piece of clingfilm and leave in the refrigerator overnight.

Grate the carrots coarsely and stir into the cabbage with the mayonnaise. Leave to stand for an hour in the refrigerator before tasting and checking the seasoning, then pile into a large serving dish.

SERVES 8

Celeriac Salad

Blanching the celeriac first means that it keeps its colour and doesn't go brown. Take care not to cook for longer than a couple of minutes, otherwise it will lose its crispness. This salad also makes a good first course.

PREPARATION TIME: 15 minutes

8 oz (225 g) celeriac, peeled
juice of ½ lemon
1 pint (600 ml) water
¼ pint (150 ml) mayonnaise (page 152)
1 level teaspoon made mustard

Cut the celeriac into thin slices, then cut each slice into fine matchsticks. Put in a saucepan with the lemon juice and water, bring quickly to the boil and simmer for 2 minutes. Drain and rinse in cold water.

Put the mayonnaise and mustard in a bowl, mix together, then stir in the celeriac. Pile into a serving dish.

SERVES 6

Potato, Apple and Celery Salad

Wash the potatoes and boil them in their skins until just tender. Drain, cool and peel off the skins. This cooking method helps the potatoes keep their shape and texture.

PREPARATION TIME: 10 minutes
CHILLING TIME: 3 hours

1 lb (450 g) cooked potatoes (see above)
3 tablespoons French dressing (page 153)
1 red-skinned eating apple
5 sticks celery, sliced
3 spring onions, shredded
salt
freshly ground black pepper
5 to 6 tablespoons mayonnaise (page 152)

Cut the potatoes into ½ inch (1.25 cm) dice, and place in a bowl with the French dressing. Toss thoroughly while they are still warm. This will give the potatoes a delicious flavour.

Core and cube the apple, and add to the potatoes with the celery, spring onions and seasoning. Cover with a plate or a piece of clingfilm, and chill well.

When ready to serve, stir in the mayonnaise, taste and check seasoning, and pile into a serving dish.

SERVES 4

Sweetcorn and Soured Cream Salad

Instead of canned sweetcorn, you can use frozen sweetcorn that has been cooked for a few minutes and then drained and cooled.

PREPARATION TIME: 5 minutes

12 oz (350 g) can sweetcorn kernels, drained
2 or 3 spring onions, finely sliced
¼ pint (150 ml) soured cream
salt
freshly ground black pepper
a few slices of red or green pepper to garnish

Put the sweetcorn into a bowl with the onions and stir in the cream. Season to taste, then pile into a small serving dish and garnish with the slices of red or green pepper around the edge of the dish.

SERVES 4

Real Mayonnaise – Fast

As you see, I use whole eggs because we like a lighter mayonnaise (if you want a rich mayonnaise, use 3 yolks and the same method). If you have not got a processor, whisk together the eggs, vinegar, sugar and seasonings, then gradually whisk in the oil until thick, and lastly add the lemon juice.

PREPARATION TIME: 10 minutes

2 eggs
1 tablespoon white wine vinegar
1 teaspoon caster sugar
1 teaspoon dry mustard
salt
freshly ground black pepper
about 1½ pints (900 ml) sunflower oil
juice of 1 large lemon

Measure all the ingredients, except the oil and lemon juice, into a processor. Switch on to blend then, with the processor running, add the oil in a slow, steady stream until the mixture is very thick and all the oil has been absorbed. Add the lemon juice and process again until thoroughly mixed. Taste and check seasoning. Put into jars, label and store in the fridge for up to a month.

MAKES about 1¾ pints (1 litre)

Variations

Herb Mayonnaise   To ½ pint (300 ml) mayonnaise add 2 tablespoons double cream and 2 tablespoons freshly chopped herbs.

Tomato Mayonnaise   For each ½ pint (300 ml) mayonnaise add about 2 level tablespoons tomato purée and a dash of Worcestershire sauce to the processor with the last of the oil.

Aioli   This is the classic French garlic mayonnaise. Add two (or more, if you like) crushed cloves of garlic to the processor with the other ingredients.

Basic French Dressing

If you choose to use sunflower oil, the dressing will be quite bland compared to a dressing made using a good olive or walnut oil – but it does cut the cost. I sometimes compromise by mixing sunflower oil with another well-flavoured oil. Of course, if you are serving a salad with a fairly highly spiced or flavoured dish, it will mask the flavour of the dressing anyway. If you make French dressing by hand, use a whisk and add the oil slowly.

PREPARATION TIME: 10 minutes

1 level teaspoon dry mustard
1 level teaspoon caster sugar
salt
freshly ground black pepper
4 to 6 tablespoons white wine or cider vinegar
¼ pint (150 ml) oil (see above)

Measure everything but the oil into a processor. Mix well then, with the processor running, add the oil slowly through the funnel until the dressing is fairly thick. Check seasoning. Store in a labelled screw-topped jar in the fridge for up to a month.

MAKES about ½ pint (300 ml)

Variations

Any of the following can be mixed with the vinegar and seasonings, before the oil is added.

Garlic Dressing   Add 2 fat cloves garlic, crushed. Serve with salads.

Herb Dressing   Add 2 tablespoons freshly chopped herbs, such as parsley, marjoram, chervil and chives. Use for tossed salads.

Basil Dressing   Add 1 tablespoon chopped fresh basil. Serve with tomatoes and summer salads.

Tarragon Dressing   Add 1 tablespoon chopped fresh tarragon. Serve with chicken.

Mint Dressing   Add 2 tablespoons chopped fresh mint. Serve with new potatoes or melon and tomato salad.

Sesame Seed Crunch

Wonderful over a salad, vegetables or rice. I am really addicted to this marvellous mixture.

4 oz (100 g) sesame seeds
8 oz (225 g) sunflower seeds
knob of butter
1 tablespoon sunflower oil
8 oz (225 g) flaked almonds

Put the seeds in a dry non-stick saucepan, cover with a lid and dry-roast over a medium heat for about 5 minutes, tossing all the time. (Keep the lid on, otherwise the seeds will pop all over the kitchen floor!)

Melt the butter in another pan, add the oil and almonds and cook until browned all over. Stir in the seeds.

Store in a jar in the fridge and use as a topping when you want to add crunch and flavour.

MAKES about 1¼ lb (550 g)

OLD-FASHIONED HOT PUDDINGS

Puddings went out of fashion some time ago – but are now rapidly coming back! They are not something I would make every day, but on a Saturday, when all the family are at home for meals, I often make a light main course and follow it up with a good old-fashioned pudding. Something else for later in the weekend can be cooked alongside the pudding while the oven is on.

Some of the puddings here reheat well, while others can also be served cold. These days I rarely serve just cream with puddings, but more often mix cream with yoghurt.

Lemon Soufflé Custard

A delicious light and easy pudding, much more special than it sounds. The top of the pudding is a spongy mousse, and the underneath a sharp lemon sauce. To make a smaller pudding, halve the quantities and bake in a 1½ pint (900 ml) dish for 30 minutes. It is also good cold – refrigerate and serve with cream.

PREPARATION AND COOKING TIME: 1 hour

4 eggs, separated
grated rind and juice of 2 large lemons
1 oz (25 g) butter
8 oz (225 g) caster sugar
2 oz (50 g) flour
16 fl oz (475 ml) milk

Heat the oven to 400°F/200°C/Gas Mark 6. Grease a 2½ pint (1.5 litre) oven-proof dish.

Put the egg yolks, lemon rind and juice, butter, sugar and flour into a processor and blend well, then add the milk through the funnel. (If you have not got a processor, work the butter and sugar together, then add the egg yolks and flour and lastly the milk.) Beat the egg whites until firm and fold into the liquid. Pour into the greased dish.

Place the dish in a roasting tin, pour boiling water into the tin to come half way up the dish, and bake for 45 minutes. Serve at once.

SERVES 8

Apple and Almond Dessert Cake

Once you've made this, you will stop making apple pie! Delicious served warm with cream. It is an excellent way of using up windfall apples, in which case you will need to start with rather more than 1 lb (450 g) fruit. If your family are not keen on almond flavoured puddings, use a little grated lemon rind in place of the almond essence.

PREPARATION AND COOKING TIME: 1¾ hours
COOLING TIME: 15 minutes

8 oz (225 g) self-raising flour
1½ level teaspoons baking powder
8 oz (225 g) caster sugar
2 large eggs
1 teaspoons almond essence
5 oz (150 g) margarine, melted
1 lb (450 g) cooking apples, peeled, cored and sliced
1 oz (25 g) flaked almonds

Heat the oven to 325°F/160°C/Gas Mark 3 and line an 8 inch (20 cm) loose-bottomed cake tin with greased greaseproof paper.

Put the flour and baking powder in a bowl with the sugar. Beat the eggs and essence together and stir them into the flour, together with the margarine, and mix well. Spread half this mixture in the tin. Arrange the apples on the cake mixture, then spoon the remaining mixture in blobs over the top of the apples. Sprinkle with the almonds.

Bake in the oven for 1½ hours until golden brown and shrinking away from the sides of the tin. Leave to cool for 15 minutes, then turn out. Serve warm, with cream.

SERVES 6

My Mother's
Bread and Butter Pudding

I don't think of this as an 'economical pudding'. In our house it is a great favourite when I know everyone is hungry. It is best left to stand, but as long as the bread is fresh it seems to work without.

PREPARATION AND COOKING TIME: 1 hour
STANDING TIME: 1 hour

about 3 oz (75 g) butter
9 thin slices white bread, crusts removed
4 oz (100 g) sultanas and currants, mixed
grated rind of 1 lemon
about 3 oz (75 g) demerara sugar
¾ pint (450 ml) milk
2 eggs

Thoroughly butter a 2½ pint (1.5 litre) ovenproof dish. Melt the butter in a saucepan and dip the bread into it, coating one side with butter (this is much easier than spreading each slice with butter). Cut each slice in three and arrange half the bread over the base of the dish, butter side down. Cover with the dried fruit, lemon rind and half the sugar, and top with the rest of the bread, butter side uppermost. Sprinkle with the remaining sugar.

Blend the milk and eggs together and pour over the pudding. Leave to stand for about an hour, then bake in a 350°F/180°C/Gas Mark 4 oven for about 40 minutes, until puffy, a pale golden brown and set.

SERVES 6

Pineapple Pudding

All made from ingredients that you are likely to have on the larder shelf, this pudding should be served warm.

PREPARATION AND COOKING TIME: 45 minutes

15 oz (425 g) can pineapple pieces
about ½ pint (300 ml) milk
2 oz (50 g) butter
2 oz (50 g) flour
4½ oz (125 g) caster sugar
2 eggs, separated

Heat the oven to 325°F/160°C/Gas Mark 3. Drain the syrup from the pineapple into a measure and make up to ¾ pint (450 ml) with milk.

Melt the butter in a saucepan, stir in the flour and cook for a minute. Add the milk mixture and bring to the boil, stirring, until the sauce has thickened. Cook for 2 minutes, then stir in 1½ oz (40 g) of the caster sugar until dissolved. Remove from the heat and beat in the egg yolks. Stir in the pineapple pieces and turn the mixture into a 2½ pint (1.5 litre) ovenproof dish.

Whisk the egg whites with an electric or hand rotary whisk until stiff, then whisk in the remaining sugar a teaspoonful at a time. Pile the meringue on top of the pineapple mixture, making sure that it comes right to the edge of the dish. Bake in the oven for about 30 minutes, until the meringue is a pale golden brown and crisp.

SERVES 4 to 6

Lemon Meringue Pie

Although this is quite difficult to get out of the dish for serving, it is really delicious and very lemony.

PREPARATION AND COOKING TIME: 50 minutes

CRUMB CRUST
6 oz (175 g) digestive biscuits
3 oz (75 g) butter
1½ oz (40 g) demerara sugar

TOPPING
3 egg whites
4½ oz (125 g) caster sugar

FILLING
grated rind and juice of 2 large
   lemons
1½ oz (40 g) cornflour
½ pint (300 ml) boiling water
2 egg yolks
3 oz (75 g) caster sugar

Put the biscuits in a polythene bag and crush with a rolling pin. Melt the butter in a small pan, add the demerara sugar and crumbs and mix well. Turn into a 9 inch (23cm) deepish flan dish and press into shape around the base and sides with the back of a spoon.

For the filling, put the lemon rind and juice in a bowl with the cornflour and blend to form a smooth paste. Bring the water to the boil in a saucepan, then pour on to the cornflour mixture. Return the cornflour to the pan, bring to the boil and simmer for 3 minutes until thick, stirring. Remove from the heat, add the egg yolks and sugar, then return to the heat for a minute to thicken the sauce. Cool slightly, then spoon the lemon filling into the flan.

Heat the oven to 325°F/160°C/Gas Mark 3. Whisk the egg whites for the topping with an electric or rotary whisk until they form stiff peaks. Add the sugar a teaspoonful at a time, whisking well after each addition. Spoon over the lemon filling, being careful to spread it right up to the edge of the crust, leaving no air spaces. Place the pie in the oven for about 30 minutes or until the meringue is a pale golden brown. Serve either warm or cold.

SERVES 6 to 8

RIGHT: *My Mother's Bread and Butter Pudding (page 158)*
OVERLEAF LEFT: *Rum and Raisin Chocolate Cheesecake (page 181)*
OVERLEAF RIGHT: *Wild Bramble Mousse (page 189)*

Treacle Tart

Treacle tart is one of those favourites that is so easy to prepare and always has the family coming back for second helpings. I try to keep breadcrumbs in the freezer so that they are easily at hand for recipes such as this.

PREPARATION AND COOKING TIME: 50 minutes

6 oz (175 g) flour
3 oz (75 g) margarine
about 2 tablespoons cold water
about 9 good tablespoons golden syrup
about 5 oz (150 g) fresh white or brown breadcrumbs
grated rind and juice of 1 large lemon

Heat the oven to 400°F/200°C/Gas Mark 6. Measure the flour into a bowl and rub in the margarine until the mixture resembles fine breadcrumbs. Add sufficient water to mix to a firm dough. Roll out thinly on a lightly floured surface and use to line a 9 inch (23 cm) deepish loose-bottomed flan tin.

Heat the syrup in a large pan until runny, then stir in the breadcrumbs, lemon rind and juice. (It may be necessary to add extra breadcrumbs if the mixture is too runny.) Turn the filling into the pastry case and level out evenly. Bake in the oven for 10 minutes, then reduce the oven temperature to 350°F/180°C/Gas Mark 4 and bake for a further 20 to 25 minutes, until the tart is cooked. Leave to cool in the tin for a few minutes, then lift out and serve in wedges.

SERVES 8

LEFT: *Old-Fashioned Rock Cakes (page 198)*

Almond Bakewell Tart

This makes a delicious tart – although it contains only almond essence, it tastes very almondy. If you prefer, make the mixture in small individual tarts (they will, of course, cook more quickly).

PREPARATION AND COOKING TIME: 1 hour
CHILLING TIME: 30 minutes

FILLING
4 oz (100 g) margarine
4 oz (100 g) caster sugar
4 oz (100 g) ground rice or semolina
½ teaspoon almond essence
1 egg, beaten
about 2 tablespoons apricot jam
a few flaked almonds

PASTRY
6 oz (175 g) flour
3 oz (75 g) margarine, cut into
  small pieces
about 2 tablespoons cold water

First make the pastry. Measure the flour into a large bowl, add the margarine and rub in until the mixture looks like crumble (the sort that you sprinkle over apples). Mix to a stiff dough with the water: add all the water at once and mix with a round-bladed knife, then gather the lump of pastry together. Rest the pastry, wrapped in clingfilm, in the refrigerator for 30 minutes.

Heat the oven to 400°F/200°C/Gas Mark 6 and put a baking sheet in the oven on the shelf just above the centre. Roll out the pastry on a floured table and use to line an 8 to 9 inch (20 to 23 cm) flan tin. Prick the base well.

To make the filling, melt the margarine in a pan and add the sugar, ground rice or semolina, almond essence and egg. Spread the base of the flan with the jam, then pour in the filling. Sprinkle the top with flaked almonds.

Bake in the oven for about 35 minutes, until the pastry is pale golden brown at the edges and the filling golden brown too. Remove from the oven and leave to cool in the flan tin for a few minutes. Serve cut into wedges.

SERVES 8

Cinnamon Apple Pancakes

The pancakes may be made and filled in advance, then reheated by frying just before serving. Alternatively, they may be put in a well-buttered tin, brushed with butter and cooked in a very hot oven for about 20 minutes, until brown. Sprinkle with cinnamon and sugar, and serve hot with cream or ice cream.

PREPARATION AND COOKING TIME: 35 minutes

4 large Bramley apples, peeled,
   cored and sliced
¼ teaspoon ground cinnamon
6 oz (175 g) demerara sugar
5 oz (150 g) butter
4 oz (100 g) flour

salt
1 egg
½ pint (300 ml) milk and water
   mixed
1 tablespoon sunflower oil, plus oil
   for frying

In a saucepan, gently cook the apples, cinnamon, sugar and 4 oz (100 g) of butter for 20 minutes, or until the apples are tender, stirring occasionally.

Meanwhile, make the pancakes. Sift the flour and salt into a bowl and make a well in the centre. Add the egg and gradually stir in half the milk and water. Using a whisk, blend in the flour from the sides of the bowl, beat well until the mixture is smooth, then stir in the remaining milk and water and the tablespoon of oil.

Heat a little oil in an 8 inch (20 cm) frying pan. When it is hot, pour off any excess oil and spoon about 2 tablespoons of batter into the pan. Tip and rotate the pan so that the batter spreads out and thinly covers the base. Cook for about a minute, until pale brown underneath, then turn over with a palette knife and cook for another minute. Slip the pancake out of the pan and set to one side, then make about seven more pancakes with the remaining batter.

Spread the pancakes flat, spoon some of the filling on to each and roll them up. In a large frying pan, heat the remaining butter with a little oil and fry the pancakes on all sides until golden brown. Pile on a warm serving dish and serve at once.

SERVES 4

Fresh Apricot and Almond Tart

Very French. Very good. If you have no vanilla sugar, use caster and add ½ teaspoon vanilla essence.

PREPARATION AND COOKING TIME: 1 hour
CHILLING TIME: 30 minutes

PASTRY
6 oz (175 g) plain flour
4 oz (100 g) butter, cut into small
  pieces
1 egg yolk
1 level tablespoon caster sugar
2 teaspoons cold water

CRÈME PÂTISSIÈRE
3 egg yolks
3 oz (75 g) vanilla sugar (page 170)
1 oz (25 g) flour
½ pint (300 ml) milk

TOPPING
1½ lb (675 g) apricots
juice of ½ lemon
6 tablespoons water
2 oz (50 g) caster sugar
1 scant teaspoon arrowroot
1 tablespoon brandy
½ oz (15 g) toasted flaked almonds

To make the pastry, put the flour in a bowl, add the butter and rub in with the fingertips until the mixture resembles fine breadcrumbs. Mix the egg yolk, sugar and water together, and stir into the dry ingredients to bind them. Roll out the pastry on a floured table, line a 9 inch (22.5 cm) flan tin and chill for 30 minutes.

Put a thick baking sheet in the oven and heat the oven to 425°F/220°C/Gas Mark 7. Line the flan with greaseproof paper and baking beans, and bake blind for 10 minutes, until beginning to brown at the edges. Remove the paper and beans and return the flan to the oven for a further 5 minutes. Cool in the tin, then carefully lift on to a serving plate.

For the crème pâtissière, put the egg yolks, sugar and flour in a bowl with a little of the milk and mix smooth with a wire whisk. Boil the rest of the milk and pour on to the yolks, whisking well. Rinse out the milk pan, then return the mixture to the pan and stir over a low heat until thickened. Remove from the heat and leave to cool, stirring occasionally. Spread in the flan case.

Wash the apricots for the topping, halve them and remove the stones. Put the lemon juice and water in a large, shallow pan. Add the apricots, cut side down, and sprinkle them with the sugar. Cover with a tight-fitting lid. Bring to the boil, then simmer until the fruit is just soft. Lift out with a slotted spoon and place on top of the crème pâtissière.

Measure the arrowroot into a bowl, add the brandy, then add the juices from the pan. Return to the pan, bring to the boil and allow the mixture to thicken. If it seems too thick to coat the fruit, thin down with a little water. Add the almonds to the glaze, then spoon over the tart to give a shiny top.

SERVES 6 to 8

Danish Cream

This is an alternative to custard and not as rich as cream. Serve very cold. A good way of using up left-over custard.

PREPARATION TIME: 3 minutes

½ pint (300 ml) thick cold custard
¼ pint (150 ml) single cream

Place the custard in a processor or blender and process until smooth. Add the cream and process again until blended. Turn into a serving dish and place in the refrigerator until very cold before serving.

MAKES ¾ pint (450 ml)

Mauritius Bananas

Fried bananas can look unexciting – with a meringue topping, they look spectacular and are very quick and easy to do. Use a lemon zester to remove the rind from the lemons.

PREPARATION AND COOKING TIME: 20 minutes

3 oz (75 g) butter
3 oz (75 g) light muscovado sugar
6 ripe bananas
rind and juice of 2 lemons
3 tablespoons rum or brandy

TOPPING
2 egg whites
4 oz (100 g) caster sugar

Heat the oven to 400°F/200°C/Gas Mark 6. Melt the butter in a large frying pan and add the muscovado sugar, cooking gently until the sugar has dissolved. Peel and thickly slice the bananas diagonally, add to the pan and toss for about 1 minute until coated. Reserve a few strips of lemon rind for decoration. Add the remaining rind and lemon juice to the pan and boil until syrupy, then add the rum or brandy. Divide between six ramekin dishes.

For the topping, whisk the egg whites until stiff, then add the sugar a teaspoonful at a time, whisking until the sugar has been incorporated. Spread over the bananas and place the ramekins in a small roasting tin.

Cook for about 5 minutes, until just beginning to colour – watch very carefully. Sprinkle with the reserved rind and serve immediately.

SERVES 6

COLD DESSERTS

All these desserts should be made ahead and chilled really well. My sort of ice cream doesn't need long softening in the refrigerator before it is served – it can come straight from freezer to table. If you are making dessert for a party or special occasion, it is nice to offer two – one light and fruity, the other rich and creamy.

Before you begin, survey your containers. For a buffet or party it's a good idea to make desserts in individual dishes or ramekins, and an attractive platter can transform a simple arrangement of fresh fruit.

Raspberry Cream Pavlova

This is really not difficult and does not take too long to make. It needs just an hour, undisturbed, in the oven. You must then turn off the heat and forget it until it is quite cold. Do not open the oven door and peep.

PREPARATION AND COOKING TIME: 1¼ hours
COOLING AND CHILLING TIME: 3 hours

3 egg whites
6 oz (175 g) caster sugar
1 teaspoon vinegar
1 level teaspoon cornflour
½ pint (300 ml) whipping cream, whipped
8 oz (225 g) fresh raspberries
a little caster sugar

Lay a sheet of silicone paper on a baking sheet and mark an 8 inch (20 cm) circle on it. Heat the oven to 325°F/160°C/Gas Mark 3.

Whisk the egg whites, with an electric or hand rotary whisk, until stiff, then whisk in the sugar a teaspoonful at a time. Blend the vinegar with the cornflour and whisk into the egg whites with the last spoonful of sugar. Spread the meringue out to cover the circle on the baking sheet, building up the sides so that they are higher than the centre.

Put the meringue case in the middle of the oven, turn the heat down to 300°F/150°C/Gas Mark 2, and bake for 1 hour. The pavlova will be a pale creamy colour rather than white. Turn the oven off and leave the pavlova undisturbed to become quite cold.

Lift the pavlova off the paper and transfer to a serving plate. Put the cream and the raspberries in a bowl, lightly fold them together and sweeten to taste with a little sugar. Pile the cream and raspberry mixture into the centre of the pavlova and leave to stand for 1 hour in a cool place or refrigerator before serving.

SERVES 6

Chocolate Roulade

A real luxury pudding. Make a day ahead, if you like, and keep chilled. Sieve more icing sugar on top before serving. Expect the roulade to crack on rolling up – this is part of its charm.

PREPARATION AND COOKING TIME: 45 minutes

3 eggs
4 oz (100 g) caster sugar
1 oz (25 g) cocoa, sieved
icing sugar
½ pint whipping cream, whipped

Heat the oven to 400°F/200°C/Gas Mark 6. Line a 9 by 13 inch (23 by 33 cm) Swiss roll tin with greased greaseproof paper.

Whisk the eggs and sugar together in a large bowl with an electric whisk, until the mixture is light and creamy and the whisk leaves a trail when lifted out. Carefully fold the cocoa into the mixture with a spoon. Turn the mixture into the tin and level out with the back of a spoon. Bake in the oven for 10 to 12 minutes, until the roulade is beginning to shrink back from the edges of the tin.

While the roulade is cooling, cut a piece of greaseproof paper a little bigger than the tin and dredge with icing sugar. When cool, invert the roulade on to the sugared paper. Quickly loosen the paper on the bottom and peel off.

To make rolling easier, trim all four edges of the roulade and make a score mark 1 inch (2.5 cm) in from one of the shorter edges, being careful not to cut right through. Spread the roulade with the cream, fold the narrow strip created by the score-mark over, and begin rolling, using the sugared paper to keep a firm roll.

Lift the roulade on to a serving plate and dust with a little more icing sugar to serve.

SERVES 4 to 6

Vanilla Ice Cream

This is an ideal stand-by to keep in the freezer. Use as a base for sundaes or parfaits, or serve with hot puddings and pies instead of custard or cream. Remove the ice cream from the freezer 5 to 10 minutes before serving, and leave to stand at room temperature. To make vanilla sugar, just store two or three vanilla pods in a screw-top jar of caster sugar. If you have not already done this, just add 1 teaspoon vanilla essence with the cream.

PREPARATION TIME: 8 minutes
FREEZING TIME: overnight

4 eggs
4 oz (100 g) vanilla sugar
½ pint (300 ml) double cream

Separate the eggs, place the yolks in a small bowl and whisk until well blended. Using a rotary or electric hand whisk, whisk the egg whites until stiff, then whisk in the sugar a teaspoonful at a time. Whisk the cream until it forms soft peaks (add the vanilla essence at this stage if no vanilla sugar is available), then fold into the egg white mixture with the egg yolks.

If you are making one of the variations on the basic ice cream (*opposite page*), the extra ingredients should be added now.

Turn the ice cream into a 2½ pint (1.5 litre) plastic container, cover and freeze overnight.

SERVES 8 to 10

Variations

If you are making one of these variations on the basic ice cream recipe, omit the vanilla sugar or vanilla essence and use plain caster sugar. Add the extra ingredients after folding in the cream and egg yolks.

Very Special Ginger Ice Cream　Add 1 level teaspoon ground ginger and 4 oz (100 g) stem ginger, chopped, to the basic ice cream.

Coffee and Brandy Ice Cream　Add 2 tablespoons coffee essence and 2 tablespoons brandy to the basic ice cream.

Fresh Lemon Ice Cream　Add the grated rind and juice of 2 lemons to the basic ice cream.

Mango Ice Cream　Add the lightly mashed flesh of a peeled and stoned mango to the basic ice cream.

Raspberry or Strawberry Ice Cream　Add ¼ pint (150 ml) strawberry purée or ¼ pint sieved raspberry purée to the basic ice cream.

Gooseberry, Plum or Rhubarb Ice Cream　Add ¼ pint (150 ml) sweetened cooked gooseberry, plum or rhubarb purée to the basic ice cream.

Tutti Frutti　Soak 4 oz (100 g) mixed chopped glacé pineapple, raisins, dried apricots, cherries and angelica overnight in 4 tablespoons brandy to plump them. Fold into the basic ice cream recipe. Serve with almond biscuits, a swirl of cream and a sprinkling of nuts.

Blackcurrant Ice Cream　Add about 3 tablespoons of blackcurrant cordial (Ribena) and 3 tablespoons cassis to the basic ice cream.

Iced Lemon Flummery

Desserts in individual dishes make serving so much simpler. Keep these ices in the freezer then, 10 minutes before serving, take them out and decorate.

PREPARATION TIME: 10 minutes
FREEZING TIME: 6 hours, then overnight

½ pint (300 ml) double cream
grated rind and juice of 2 lemons
12 oz (350 g) caster sugar
1 pint (600 ml) milk
¼ pint (150 ml) whipping cream, whipped
sprigs of fresh mint or lemon balm

Pour the double cream into a bowl and whisk until it forms soft peaks. Stir in the lemon rind, juice, sugar and milk and mix well until thoroughly blended. Pour into a 2½ pint (1.5 litre) plastic container, cover with a lid and freeze for at least 6 hours, until firm.

Cut into chunks and process in a processor or blender until smooth and creamy. Pour into individual ramekin dishes and return to the freezer overnight.

To serve, pipe a small blob of cream on top of each ramekin and decorate with a sprig of mint or lemon balm.

SERVES 8 to 12

Bergen Lemon Cream

I first made this when I was Cookery Editor of *Ideal Home* magazine, and I still get letters from people who continue to make it. It's very simple, and a good way of using up broken meringues.

PREPARATION TIME: 8 minutes

½ pint (300 ml) double cream
finely grated rind and juice of 3 lemons
2 oz (50 g) caster sugar
2 egg whites
3 large meringues (page 204), broken in pieces

Put the cream, lemon rind and juice in a bowl with the sugar, and whisk the mixture until it forms soft peaks. In another bowl, whisk the egg whites until they form stiff peaks.

Fold the egg whites into the cream mixture with the broken meringues. Turn into six individual dishes to serve.

SERVES 6

Scotch Mist

Another way with broken meringues. Guests will probably think you've spent hours preparing this, but it only takes a few minutes. Whisk ½ pint (300 ml) double cream with 3 tablespoons whisky until the mixture holds its shape. Lightly crush 2 oz (50 g) meringues (*page 204*) in a plastic bag, then fold into the cream. Spoon into small, stemmed glasses and chill for about an hour before serving decorated with sugared almonds.

SERVES 4

Passion Pudding

Otherwise known as Barbados Cream – I have called it both these names over the past few years! The easiest pudding to make and not as wicked as cream alone. Individual dishes are a good idea when you have a choice of desserts: I make these in ramekins or syllabub cups.

PREPARATION TIME: 10 minutes
CHILLING TIME: overnight

½ pint (300 ml) double cream
1 pint (600 ml) natural yoghurt
soft brown sugar

Lightly whip the cream, blend in the yoghurt and turn into a 1½ pint (900 ml) glass dish or six small ramekin dishes. Sprinkle with a ¼ inch (5 mm) layer of sugar.

Put in the refrigerator and chill overnight. Sprinkle again with sugar before serving well chilled.

SERVES 6

Lemon Syllabub

This is a simple rich sweet that I like to serve with shortbread biscuits.

PREPARATION TIME: 5 minutes

½ pint (300 ml) double cream
finely grated rind and juice of 1 lemon
1 tablespoon brandy
1 tablespoon sherry
2 oz (50 g) caster sugar

Place all the ingredients together in a bowl and whisk until light but not thick. Serve in small glasses or syllabub cups.

SERVES 4

Kiwi Syllabub

For an attractive and refreshing variation on the basic syllabub, peel and slice 3 kiwi fruit and use the slices to line four tall glasses (this takes a little time). Prepare the syllabub mixture as described above and spoon it into the glasses.

SERVES 4

Caramel Syllabub

The breadcrumbs and syllabub can be separately prepared well ahead, and then just stirred together when required. Serve with brandy snaps.

PREPARATION AND COOKING TIME: 15 minutes

3 oz (75 g) fresh brown breadcrumbs
3 oz (75 g) muscovado sugar
¾ pint (450 ml) double cream
grated rind and juice of 1 lemon
2 tablespoons brandy
2 tablespoons sherry

Place the breadcrumbs and muscovado sugar on a piece of foil and toast under a hot grill until golden brown and caramelised, stirring occasionally. Keep a watchful eye on the crumbs while they are browning, and wait for them to turn a dark chestnut colour. This will take about 6 minutes or so. Leave to become cold.

Measure all the remaining ingredients into a bowl and whisk until light, but not thick.

To serve, stir the breadcrumbs into the syllabub and spoon into six tall serving glasses.

SERVES 6

St. Andrew's Layer

An easy cold pudding that tastes good and is very rich. Sometimes I make this in small wine glasses. It looks attractive, as you can see the layers clearly.

PREPARATION TIME: 10 minutes
CHILLING TIME: 6 hours

4 oz (100 g) fresh white or brown breadcrumbs
3 oz (75 g) demerara sugar
8 level tablespoons drinking chocolate
2 level tablespoons instant coffee
½ pint (300 ml) double cream
¼ pint (150 ml) single cream
2 oz (50 g) plain chocolate, coarsely grated

Place the breadcrumbs, sugar, drinking chocolate and coffee in a bowl and mix thoroughly. Put the creams in another bowl and whisk together until they form soft peaks.

Put half the cream in the base of a 2 pint (1.2 litre) shallow dish, cover with the chocolate crumbs and then with the remaining cream. Smooth the top and leave in the refrigerator for at least 6 hours.

Cover the top with grated chocolate just before serving.

SERVES 6

Small Caramel Custards

Leave in the ramekin dishes or cups until the last moment before turning out, otherwise the caramel topping loses its shine and colour. Serve very cold. Make a large crème caramel in a 1¾ pint (1 litre) soufflé dish and bake in the oven for about 1½ hours. If you have no vanilla sugar, use 2 oz (50 g) caster sugar and add a few drops of vanilla essence to the custard.

PREPARATION AND COOKING TIME: 60 minutes
COOLING TIME: 12 hours

3 oz (75 g) granulated sugar
3 tablespoons water
5 eggs
2 oz (50 g) vanilla sugar (page 170)
1¼ pints (750 ml) milk

To make the caramel, put the granulated sugar and water in a heavy saucepan and dissolve over a low heat. Bring to the boil and boil until the syrup is a pale golden brown. Remove from the heat and quickly pour into six small ramekins.

For the custard, first mix the eggs and vanilla sugar together. Warm the milk in a saucepan over a low heat until it is hand hot, then pour it on to the egg mixture, stirring constantly.

Butter the sides of the ramekins above the caramel. Strain the custard into the ramekins, and place in a roasting tin half filled with hot water. Bake in the oven at 300°F/150°C/Gas Mark 2 for 45 to 60 minutes, or until set.

Remove the caramel custards from the oven and leave to cool and set for at least 12 hours or overnight. Turn out on to individual dishes to serve.

SERVES 6

Real Crème Brûlée

Expensive to make, but quick and a real luxury. Just sprinkle with demerara sugar, slip under the grill and brown a couple of hours before serving, then chill well.

PREPARATION AND COOKING TIME: 1¼ hours
CHILLING TIME: overnight, plus 2 hours

1 egg
3 egg yolks
¾ pint (450 ml) single cream
1½ oz (40 g) caster sugar
a few drops of vanilla essence
2 to 3 oz (50 to 75 g) demerara sugar

Heat the oven to 300°F/150°C/Gas Mark 2. Blend the egg, yolks, cream, caster sugar and vanilla essence together and turn into an ovenproof dish. Stand in a meat tin containing 1 inch (2.5 cm) hot water and bake in the oven for about 1 hour, or until just firm. Remove from the oven and cool, then leave in the refrigerator overnight.

A couple of hours before serving, sprinkle the top with the demerara sugar and brown under a hot grill for 3 to 4 minutes, until the sugar has melted and become crisp. Serve chilled.

SERVES 4

Mocha Pots

A very rich pudding, so serve after a fairly light meal.

PREPARATION AND COOKING TIME: 15 minutes
CHILLING TIME: 1 hour

1 oz (25 g) butter
6 oz (175 g) plain chocolate, broken into squares
2 tablespoons rum
3 teaspoons instant coffee dissolved in 1 tablespoon hot water
4 eggs, separated
¼ pint (150 ml) whipping cream, whipped

Put the butter and chocolate in a bowl over a pan of simmering water and allow to melt. Add the rum and coffee. Stir in the egg yolks and mix well. Remove from the heat and allow to cool.

Whisk the egg whites with an electric or rotary whisk until they form peaks. Gently fold in the chocolate mixture, then pour into six ramekin dishes. Chill in the fridge until set, then decorate with a swirl of whipped cream just before serving.

SERVES 6

Rum and Raisin
Chocolate Cheesecake

Quite a long recipe, but well worth making it for a special occasion. Start the night before by soaking the raisins in the rum.

PREPARATION AND COOKING TIME: 30 minutes
CHILLING TIME: 6 hours

2½ oz (65 g) butter
2 oz (50 g) demerara sugar
5 oz (150 g) digestive biscuits,
  crushed
¼ pint (150 ml) whipping cream
chocolate flake or drops to decorate

FILLING
1 teaspoon instant coffee
2 level tablespoons cocoa

3 tablespoons boiling water
2 eggs, separated
2 oz (50 g) caster sugar
½ oz (15 g) powdered gelatine
3 tablespoons cold water
8 oz (225 g) cream cheese
¼ pint (150 ml) whipping cream,
  lightly whipped
2 oz (50 g) raisins soaked overnight
  in 4 tablespoons rum

Melt the butter and stir in the demerara sugar and biscuit crumbs until blended. Press into a 9 inch (23 cm) flan dish, and put in the refrigerator to harden.

Meanwhile, prepare the filling. In a bowl, mix the coffee and cocoa with the boiling water, then add the egg yolks and caster sugar. Place the bowl over a pan of hot water and stir until the mixture thickens to coat the back of a spoon (about 10 minutes). Remove from the heat.

Put the gelatine in a small bowl with the water and leave to stand for about 3 minutes to form a 'sponge', then stand the bowl over a pan of simmering water until the gelatine has become quite clear. Remove from the heat and stir into the coffee and cocoa mixture. In a large bowl, beat the cream cheese until soft, then gradually stir in the cooled cocoa mixture and the cream. Add the rum and raisins and pour the mixture into the flan case.

Chill the cheesecake in the refrigerator until set, then whip the cream and decorate the cheesecake with whipped cream and chocolate.

SERVES 8

Grapefruit Cheesecake

This cheesecake is sharp, rich and creamy. To turn out, dip the tin in a bowl of very hot water for a moment, then put a serving plate on top of the tin and invert. Lift the tin off the cheesecake, peel off the circle of greaseproof paper and decorate as suggested in the recipe. This method means that you get a crisp base to the cheesecake and you do not need to buy a springform tin.

PREPARATION AND COOKING TIME: 30 minutes
CHILLING TIME: overnight

½ oz (15 g) gelatine
3 tablespoons cold water
1 lb (450 g) cream cheese
6 oz (175 g) can frozen concentrated unsweetened
 grapefruit juice, thawed
3 oz (75 g) caster sugar
½ pint (300 ml) whipping cream
4 oz (100 g) ginger biscuits
2 oz (50 g) butter
1 oz (25 g) demerara sugar
black and white seedless grapes to decorate

Place the gelatine in a small basin with the water and leave to stand for 3 minutes to form a 'sponge', then stand the bowl over a pan of simmering water until the gelatine has become clear. Remove from the heat and leave to cool.

Cream the cheese until soft, then gradually beat in the grapefruit juice and caster sugar. Stir in the cooled gelatine. Whisk the cream until it is thick but not stiff, and fold into the cheese. Place a circle of greaseproof paper in the bottom of a lightly oiled 8 inch (20 cm) cake tin and turn the cheesecake mixture into the tin. Place in the refrigerator.

Crush the biscuits finely. Melt the butter in a pan and stir in the biscuit crumbs and demerara sugar. Press this mixture over the cheesecake, and return to the refrigerator for several hours – preferably overnight.

Turn out the cheesecake on to a serving plate and remove the greaseproof paper. Decorate the top with halved black and white grapes.

SERVES 8

Lemon Cheesecake

Decorate the top of this cheesecake with fruits that are in season – grapes, sliced kiwi fruit, strawberries – or with sugared lemon slices.

PREPARATION AND COOKING TIME: 15 minutes
CHILLING TIME: overnight

3 oz (75 g) digestive biscuits
1½ oz (40 g) butter
1 oz (25 g) demerara sugar
8 oz (225 g) cream cheese
14 oz (397 g) can condensed milk
grated rind and juice of 3 lemons
¼ pint (150 ml) soured cream
fresh seasonal fruit to decorate

Place the biscuits in a polythene bag and crush with a rolling pin. Melt the butter in a small saucepan, add the sugar and biscuit crumbs, and mix well. Turn into an 8 inch (20 cm) loose-bottomed cake tin and press firmly on to the base with the back of a spoon.

Put the cream cheese into a bowl and cream well until soft, then beat in the condensed milk until smooth. Mix in the lemon rind and juice. Pour over the biscuit base, smooth, and chill in the refrigerator until set – preferably overnight.

Loosen the sides of the tin, press up the base and lift the cheesecake on to a flat dish. Spread the top with the soured cream and decorate with fruit.

SERVES 6 to 8

Griestorte with Pineapple and Ginger

Provided that you have a small electric hand mixer or a strong right arm and a whisk, this is very quick to make.

PREPARATION AND COOKING TIME: 45 minutes

3 eggs, separated
4 oz (100 g) caster sugar
½ teaspoon almond essence
2 oz (50 g) semolina
½ oz (15 g) ground almonds

FILLING
8 oz (227 g) can of pineapple
¼ pint (150 ml) double cream
a little preserved stem ginger, finely chopped

Heat the oven to 350°F/180°C/Gas Mark 4. Grease and line an 8 inch (20 cm) round cake tin with greased greaseproof paper and dust with flour.

Put the egg yolks and sugar in a bowl over a pan of hot water and whisk until the mixture is pale and thick. Remove from the heat, then fold in the almond essence, semolina and ground almonds. Whisk the egg whites until they form soft peaks, and fold into the mixture. Turn into the cake tin and bake in the oven for about 30 minutes, or until the cake is well risen and pale golden brown. Turn out, remove the paper and leave to cool on a wire rack. Split the cake in half horizontally when it is completely cold.

For the filling, drain the pineapple thoroughly and then chop finely. Whisk the cream until thick, then stir in the pineapple and a little stem ginger. Use the cream mixture to sandwich the cake together. Place on a serving dish and sprinkle with sugar, if you like.

SERVES 8

Thomas's Flan

This is a flan the children could make themselves. It is named after my elder son who makes it regularly. Decorate it with any fruit that is to hand: grapes are nice, or strawberries or raspberries, and in winter canned mandarin oranges look very good.

PREPARATION AND COOKING TIME: 10 minutes
CHILLING TIME: 4 hours

2 oz (50 g) butter or margarine
1 level tablespoon demerara sugar
8 digestive biscuits, crushed

FILLING
6 oz (196 g) can condensed milk
¼ pint (150 ml) double cream
juice of 2 lemons
fruit to decorate

Melt the butter or margarine in a saucepan, remove from the heat and stir in the sugar and crushed biscuits. Mix well and press the mixture over the base and sides of a 7 inch (17.5 cm) flan ring or a loose-bottomed flan tin. Spread evenly, using a metal tablespoon.

Put the condensed milk, cream and lemon juice in a bowl and whisk the mixture together until well blended. Pour into the flan case. Chill in the refrigerator for several hours.

When ready to serve, remove the flan ring and decorate the top of the flan with fruit.

SERVES 4 to 6

Brandy Chocolate Charlotte

If brandy isn't a top favourite, dip the sponge fingers in unsweetened orange juice.

PREPARATION AND COOKING TIME: 20 minutes
CHILLING TIME: overnight

3 tablespoons brandy
about 17 sponge fingers
4 oz (100 g) plain chocolate
2 eggs
6 oz (175 g) soft unsalted butter
5 oz (150 g) caster sugar
1/4 pint (150 ml) whipping cream, whipped until thick
a few Maltesers to decorate

Dip each sponge finger, sugar side down, in the brandy and arrange 9 or 10 fingers, sugar side down, on the base of a 2 lb (900 g) loaf tin. Cut the remaining sponge fingers in half and dip, sugar side down, in the brandy and stand, sugar side out, around the sides of the tin.

Break the chocolate into pieces, place in a small bowl over a pan of simmering water and allow to melt slowly. Put the melted chocolate, eggs, butter and sugar in a processor, and blend until smooth. (Alternatively, beat well with an electric mixer). Turn the mixture into the loaf tin and smooth the top. Chill overnight.

Turn out the charlotte on to a serving dish and decorate with piped cream rosettes and Maltesers.

SERVES 8

Chocolate Juliet

This chocolate loaf is very rich, so serve it in thin slices – with cream! Use plain chocolate if you prefer.

PREPARATION AND COOKING TIME: 10 minutes
CHILLING TIME: overnight

7 oz (200 g) milk chocolate
8 oz (225 g) hard margarine
2 eggs
1 oz (25 g) caster sugar
8 oz (225 g) Nice biscuits
¼ pint (150 ml) double cream, whipped
chocolate buttons, Matchmakers or chocolate-coated mints to decorate

Line a 7½ by 4 by 2½ inch (19 by 10 by 6 cm) loaf tin with foil. Break the chocolate into small pieces and place in a saucepan with the margarine. Heat gently until the mixture has melted. Beat the eggs and sugar together in a bowl until blended, then add the chocolate mixture, a little at a time. Break the biscuits into ½ inch (1.25 cm) pieces and stir into the chocolate mixture. Pack into the tin and smooth the top.

Leave the dessert to set in the refrigerator overnight, until quite firm. Just before serving, turn out on to a serving dish and peel off the foil. Decorate with cream and chocolates.

SERVES 8

Refreshing Lemon Mousse

Great for a party – either make two, or make one very big mousse in a 4 pint (2.4 litre) dish.

PREPARATION TIME: 20 minutes
CHILLING TIME: at least 4 hours

4 eggs, separated
4 oz (100 g) caster sugar
grated rind and juice of 2 large lemons
½ oz (15 g) powdered gelatine
3 tablespoons cold water
whipped cream, lemon slices and mint to decorate

Put the egg yolks in a bowl with the sugar and beat until well blended and creamy, then add the lemon rind and juice. Put the whites in a separate bowl ready for whisking.

Place the gelatine and water in a small bowl and leave for about 3 minutes to form a 'sponge'. Allow the gelatine to dissolve over a pan of simmering water, cool slightly and stir into the yolk mixture. Leave to cool but not set.

Whisk the egg whites, using an electric hand whisk, until stiff, then fold into the lemon mixture. Pour into a 2 pint (1.2 litre) glass dish and chill in the refrigerator until set. Decorate with whipped cream, lemon slices and mint.

SERVES 8 to 10

Wild Bramble Mousse

Prepare the mousse in individual ramekin dishes the day before, then turn out on to serving dishes half an hour before serving and decorate as suggested. The mousses will stand for some time once decorated, but the longer they are left to stand the darker a shade of pink the cream will become. If you like, reserve a few whole blackberries for decoration.

PREPARATION AND COOKING TIME: 30 minutes
CHILLING TIME: 6 hours

1½ lb (675 g) blackberries
6 oz (175 g) caster sugar
juice of ½ large lemon
½ oz (15 g) powdered gelatine

3 tablespoons cold water
¼ pint (150 ml) double cream
2 egg whites
¼ pint (150 ml) single cream

Put the blackberries in a pan with the sugar and lemon juice. Cover and cook over a low heat for about 15 minutes, until the blackberries are soft and the juice is beginning to run out. Purée in a processor or blender, then sieve to remove the seeds. Pour two thirds of the purée into a large bowl and reserve the remaining third for decoration.

Put the gelatine and water in a small bowl and leave to stand for about 3 minutes to form a 'sponge'. Set the bowl over a pan of simmering water until the gelatine has dissolved, then allow to cool slightly. Stir the gelatine into the large bowl of fruit purée and leave on one side until cold and just beginning to thicken.

Lightly whisk the double cream until it forms soft peaks and whisk the egg whites with an electric whisk until they form peaks. Fold them both into the slightly thickened purée until blended. Spoon the mixture into individual ramekin dishes and chill until set.

Turn out the mousses on to flat serving plates (dip the ramekins in hot water for a second, if necessary, to help loosen the mousse) and pour a little of the reserved purée around each mousse. Pour the single cream into a greaseproof paper piping bag, snip the end and trail three rings of cream around each mousse on top of the purée. Drag a fine skewer carefully in lines about 1 inch (2.5 cm) apart from the mousse to the edge of the purée, then between these lines drag the skewer in the opposite direction, from the edge of the purée to the mousse, to give a 'feathering' effect. Serve as soon as possible.

SERVES 6 to 8

An Exceedingly Good Summer Pudding

This is a recipe I am including because it really is simple and quick to make, and so delicious. If you have an abundance of these fruits, either make two puddings and freeze one or make a Red Fruit Salad: serve the cooked fruits really cold with cream.

PREPARATION AND COOKING TIME: 15 minutes
CHILLING TIME: overnight

6 to 8 large fairly thick slices white bread, crusts removed
8 oz (225 g) rhubarb, cut into ½ inch (1.25 cm) lengths
8 oz (225 g) blackberries
4 oz (100 g) blackcurrants
8 oz (225 g) redcurrants
12 oz (350 g) granulated sugar
6 tablespoons water
8 oz (225 g) small strawberries, hulled
8 oz (225 g) raspberries, hulled
thick cream to serve

Put one slice of bread aside for the top and use the remainder to line the base and sides of a 2½ pint (1.5 litre) basin (or use a round, fairly shallow dish).

Put the rhubarb, blackberries and currants into a saucepan, and add the sugar and water. Bring to the boil and simmer for a few minutes until barely tender, stirring. Add the strawberries and raspberries and cook for a further minute.

Turn the fruits into the basin, saving a small bowlful to spoon over the top of the pudding when serving. Lay the reserved slice of bread on top of the fruits and bend over the tops of the bread slices at the sides towards the centre. Place a saucer on top, pressing down a little until the juices rise to the top of the basin.

Leave the pudding to soak until cold, then put in the refrigerator overnight. Turn out just before serving and top with the reserved fruits. Serve with lots of thick cream.

SERVES 8

Exotic Fresh Fruits

Chill all the fruits for several hours before you begin.

PREPARATION TIME: 20 minutes

1 ripe melon
1 pawpaw
1 small perfect pineapple
1 mango
2 kiwi fruits
8 oz (225 g) strawberries, hulled
2 small bunches grapes

Cut the melon in half, scoop out the seeds, cut into slim wedges and remove the peel from each. Peel the pawpaw, halve and remove the seeds, and cut in wedges. Leaving the top on the pineapple, very thinly peel the fruit then, with a sharp knife, cut out the brown 'eyes' (they actually run in lines around the pineapple and so give a spiral effect when cut out in long lines). Slice the pineapple into rings, then reassemble the fruit. Peel the mango, cut through either side of the stone, then cut the flesh into wedges. Peel and slice the kiwi fruits.

Arrange the melon, pawpaw, mango and kiwi fruits around a serving platter, keeping each type grouped together and leaving a space in the middle. Stand the pineapple at the back of the platter. Just before serving, put the strawberries and grapes in the centre.

SERVES 8 (or more!)

Peaches and Strawberries with Orange

A simple, refreshing dessert.

PREPARATION TIME: 20 minutes
CHILLING TIME: 3 hours

4 fresh peaches
juice of 1 orange
1 lb (450 g) small strawberries
3 oz (75 g) caster sugar

Cut the peaches in half and remove the stones. Peel, slice into the bottom of a glass serving dish and cover immediately with the orange juice. Hull and slice the strawberries and arrange on top of the peaches. Sprinkle with the caster sugar, cover with clingfilm and chill in the refrigerator for several hours before serving.

To serve, gently mix the two fruits so that they are evenly blended.

SERVES 6

RIGHT: *Coffee Fudge Bars (page 200)*
OVERLEAF LEFT: *Chocolate Cake Tray Bake (pages 202–203)*
OVERLEAF RIGHT: *All-in-One Victoria Sandwich with Chocolate and Coffee variations (pages 206–207)*

Caramelised Oranges

An easy and refreshing pudding for a buffet party, and it can be prepared the night before. If you like, add a little orange liqueur such as Grand Marnier.

PREPARATION AND COOKING TIME: 30 minutes
CHILLING TIME: overnight

8 seedless oranges
4 whole cloves
12 oz (350 g) granulated sugar
½ pint (300 ml) water

Thinly pare the rind from two of the oranges, cut it into thin strips, then place in a pan and cover with cold water. Bring to the boil and allow to simmer for 2 minutes, until tender, then drain the rind and reserve the liquid.

With a sharp knife, cut all the peel and pith off the oranges, then cut the flesh across into about six slices. Reassemble the slices in orange shapes and save all the juice. Stand the oranges in individual serving dishes or stand in a large heatproof bowl so they are just touching. Add the cloves.

Measure the sugar into a pan with the water, heat gently until the sugar has dissolved, then increase heat and boil rapidly for 2 minutes to give a thin syrup. Remove from the heat and add the reserved orange juice and 2 tablespoons of the liquid in which the rind was boiled. Pour over the oranges, sprinkle with the thin strips of rind, and allow to cool.

Cover with clingfilm and chill overnight in the refrigerator before serving.

SERVES 8

LEFT: *Superb Carrot Cake (page 219)*

Four Seasons
Fresh Fruit Dessert Cake

I have called this 'Four Seasons' as you can substitute different fillings depending on the time of year.

PREPARATION AND COOKING TIME: 45 minutes

6 eggs
6 oz (175 g) caster sugar, warmed
6 oz (175 g) self-raising flour
a little sieved icing sugar
sprig of fresh mint or lemon balm

FILLING
pineapple jam
1 whole small fresh pineapple,
*   skinned, cored and chopped*
1 small punnet raspberries, hulled
½ pint (300 ml) whipping cream

Heat the oven to 350°F/180°C/Gas Mark 4. Grease a 10 inch (25 cm) deep round cake tin and line with a circle of greased greaseproof paper.

Pour nearly boiling water into the bowl of an electric mixer with the beaters in, then pour away the water; this heats both the bowl and the beaters. Break the eggs into the heated bowl and whisk in the sugar until the mixture is light and creamy and will leave a trail when the whisk is lifted out. Carefully fold in the flour until evenly blended.

Pour the mixture into the lined tin and bake in the oven for about 35 minutes, until the top of the cake springs back when lightly pressed with a finger. Turn out and leave to cool on a wire rack. Meanwhile, whip the cream.

Split the sponge in half and spread both halves with the jam. Reserve a few raspberries for decoration and mix the remainder with the pineapple and cream. Use to sandwich the two halves of the cake together. Lift on to a serving plate, dredge with a little icing sugar, and decorate with a sprig of fresh mint or lemon balm and the reserved raspberries.

SERVES 10

Old English Trifle

Trifle is something that has gone very much out of fashion these days, but I welcome it back. It is best made in a shallow glass dish. If time is short, make thick custard using custard powder and the top of the milk, then whisk well in a processor or blender – the result will be beautifully creamy and the colour and texture lighter.

PREPARATION AND COOKING TIME: 25 minutes
CHILLING TIME: 30 minutes

8 oz (225 g) can pears
6 individual sponge cakes, split in half
strawberry jam
2 oz (50 g) ratafia biscuits
12 maraschino cherries, chopped
1 tablespoon maraschino syrup
5 tablespoons sherry
¼ pint (150 ml) whipping cream
½ oz (15 g) blanched almonds, split and lightly toasted

CUSTARD
3 egg yolks
1 oz (25 g) caster sugar
1 heaped teaspoon cornflour
½ pint (300 ml) milk

Drain the pears, reserving the juice, then cut the fruit into small pieces. Sandwich the sponge cakes together with the strawberry jam. Put with the pears on the bottom of a shallow 2 pint (1.2 litre) serving dish and top with the ratafia biscuits. Sprinkle over the chopped cherries, pear juice, maraschino syrup and sherry.

For the custard, mix together the egg yolks, sugar and cornflour. Warm the milk in a saucepan over a low heat until it is hand-hot, then pour it on to the yolk mixture, stirring constantly. Return the mixture to the saucepan and cook gently, stirring until it thickens. Do not allow to boil, otherwise the custard will curdle. Allow to cool, then pour over the sponge cakes and chill until set.

Lightly whisk the cream until it is thick, then spread it over the custard. Spike with the almonds and serve.

SERVES 6

FAMILY CAKES

These are all my favourite recipes! Perhaps my most popular book is *Fast Cakes*, and I now make nearly all my cakes by the put-everything-in-the-bowl-together method – it really makes life so easy. Most cakes freeze extremely well, but to enjoy them at their best eat them within three months. Wrap cakes in clingfilm, then in foil or put them in a polythene box before freezing.

It's worth having really good non-stick tins to bake in. Otherwise, if they are not reliably non-stick, line them with greased greaseproof paper, or go for loose-bottomed tins.

Coffee and Chocolate Éclairs

These are quite one of my most favourite things to eat. The coffee filling makes them that extra bit more special. Be sure to dry out the pastry cases thoroughly during the baking before filling with cream, so that they are crisp to eat. Ideally, they should be filled just before serving so that they retain this crispiness.

PREPARATION AND COOKING TIME: 1 hour

2 oz (50 g) butter
¼ pint (150 ml) water
2½ oz (65 g) flour
2 eggs, beaten

TOPPING
2 oz (50 g) plain chocolate
2 tablespoons water
½ oz (15 g) butter
3 oz (75 g) icing sugar, sieved

FILLING
2 oz (50 g) icing sugar, sieved
1 tablespoon coffee essence
½ pint (300 ml) whipping cream,
  whipped

Heat the oven to 425°F/220°C/Gas Mark 7 and grease two large baking sheets.

To make the pastry, measure the butter and water into a pan, slowly bring to the boil and allow the butter to melt. Remove from the heat and add the flour all at once, then beat until it forms a soft ball. Gradually add the eggs, a little at a time, beating well to give a smooth, shiny paste. Put the mixture into a piping bag fitted with a ½ inch (1.25 cm) plain nozzle, and pipe 20 éclairs on to the baking sheets, leaving room for them to expand during cooking.

Bake in the oven for 10 minutes, then reduce the temperature to 375°F/190°C/Gas Mark 5 and cook for a further 15 to 20 minutes, until well risen and golden brown. Remove from the oven and split one side of each éclair with a knife to allow the steam to escape.

For the filling, fold the icing sugar and coffee essence into the cream. Pipe or spoon the cream into the éclairs. For the topping, put the chocolate, water and butter in a bowl and heat gently over a pan of simmering water until the mixture has melted. Remove from the heat and beat in the icing sugar until smooth. Pour into a shallow dish and dip each éclair into the sauce to coat the top. Allow to set on a cake rack before serving.

MAKES 20 éclairs

Old-Fashioned Rock Cakes

These cakes take no time at all to prepare, and are wonderful to serve if you have unexpected guests. They are best eaten when freshly made.

PREPARATION AND COOKING TIME: 25 minutes

8 oz (225 g) self-raising flour
1 good teaspoon baking powder
½ level teaspoon ground mixed spice
4 oz (100 g) soft margarine
2 oz (50 g) demerara sugar
4 oz (100 g) mixed dried fruit
1 egg, beaten
about 1 tablespoon milk
a little extra demerara sugar, for topping

Heat the oven to 400°F/200°C/Gas Mark 6. Lightly grease two large baking sheets.

Measure the flour, baking powder and mixed spice into a bowl and rub in the margarine until the mixture resembles fine breadcrumbs. Add the sugar and fruit and mix to a stiff dough with the egg and milk, adding a little extra milk if the dough is too dry.

Spoon the mixture in rough mounds on the baking sheets using two teaspoons, sprinkle with a little demerara sugar and bake in the oven for about 15 minutes, until just beginning to turn golden brown. Carefully lift off the baking sheet with a metal spatula and leave to cool on a cake rack.

MAKES 16 cakes

Jelly Tot Cakes

These tiny cakes are made in *petits fours* paper cases. They are so small that children can eat several at a time and seem to enjoy the novelty of them more than a large fairy cake or bun. They also enjoy helping to make them, particularly putting the sweets on top. Use Smarties or other small sweets instead of Jelly Tots, if you prefer.

PREPARATION AND COOKING TIME: 40 minutes

3 oz (75 g) soft margarine
2 eggs, beaten
4 oz (100 g) self-raising flour
1 level teaspoon baking powder
3 oz (75 g) caster sugar
1 tablespoon milk
Jelly Tots to decorate

ICING
4 oz (100 g) icing sugar, sieved
about 1 tablespoon lemon juice

Heat the oven to 350°F/180°C/Gas Mark 4. Arrange 50 *petits fours* cases on baking sheets.

Measure the margarine, eggs, flour, baking powder, sugar and milk into a bowl and beat well until thoroughly blended. Spoon scant teaspoonfuls of the mixture into the cases. (Be careful not to overfill the cases as the mixture will rise during baking.) Bake in the oven for 15 to 20 minutes, until well risen and pale golden brown. Cool on cake racks.

For the icing, put the icing sugar in a bowl and add sufficient lemon juice to give a spreading consistency. Spoon a little on top of each cake and spread out with the back of the spoon. When the icing has almost set, top with a Jelly Tot.

MAKES 50 tiny cakes

Coffee Fudge Bars

These bars have a very mild coffee flavour which, strangely enough, is popular with children. You can leave out the nuts but the result will not be quite as good.

PREPARATION AND COOKING TIME: 50 minutes

6 oz (175 g) soft margarine
6 oz (175 g) caster sugar
3 large eggs
4 oz (100 g) shelled walnuts, chopped
1 tablespoon coffee essence
6 oz (175 g) self-raising flour
1½ level teaspoons baking powder

ICING
3 oz (75 g) soft margarine
8 oz (225 g) icing sugar, sieved
1 tablespoon milk
1 tablespoon coffee essence

Heat the oven to 325°F/160°C/Gas Mark 3 and grease and line with greased greaseproof paper a 12 by 9 inch (30 by 23 cm) tin. Alternatively, line the tin with foil (*page 202*).

Measure the margarine, sugar, eggs, half the walnuts and the coffee essence into a bowl, then sieve in the flour and baking powder. Beat well until smooth and blended. Turn into the prepared tin and smooth the top. Bake for 40 minutes, or until the cake is well risen and shrinking away from the sides of the tin. The cake should spring back when lightly pressed with the fingertips. Leave to cool in the tin.

For the icing, put the margarine, icing sugar, milk and coffee essence in a bowl and beat until smooth. Spread over the cake and sprinkle with the remaining walnuts. Cut into bars.

MAKES 20 bars

Caramel Crunch Bars

Annabel and her friends make these often. Each time it means a trip to the village post office just to get the caramels and marshmallows! The young love to eat these bars instead of cakes or biscuits and I find that they are also very popular accompaniments to ice cream or mousse. You can cut down the recipe and only make a half quantity, but in our house they are so popular and useful that it never seems worthwhile making less.

PREPARATION TIME: 10 minutes

4 oz (100 g) margarine
4 oz (100 g) marshmallows
4 oz (100 g) caramels
7 oz (200 g) Rice Krispies

Put the margarine, marshmallows and caramels in a saucepan and heat gently over a moderate heat until the mixture is melted and smooth. (Be patient: this will take about 5 minutes.)

Meanwhile, put the Rice Krispies in a large bowl. Remove the pan from the heat, pour all at once on to the Rice Krispies and stir very thoroughly until they are well and evenly coated.

Spoon into a 12 by 9 inch (30 by 23 cm) tin and press flat. Leave in a cool place until set and quite firm, then cut into bars.

MAKES 21 bars

Tray Bakes

A really good recipe, perfect for large families, coffee mornings, bazaars and school fêtes. I have suggested lining the tin with foil: you can lift it out of the tin complete with cake, ready to ice. It also leaves the tin free if you want to make another one. Of course, if you wish, don't line the tin with foil but just grease it – bake in the tin, ice in the tin and then cut slices and lift out with a palate knife.

PREPARATION AND COOKING TIME: 50 minutes

6 oz (175 g) soft margarine
8 oz (225 g) self-raising flour
1½ level teaspoons baking powder
6 oz (175 g) caster sugar
3 eggs
3 tablespoons milk

Heat the oven to 350°F/180°C/Gas Mark 4. Take a meat roasting tin about 12 by 9 inches (30 by 23 cm), turn it upside down, then mould a larger piece of foil over the tin, smoothing it with your hands, to make a foil case. Use this foil case as a lining inside the roasting tin. Grease well before adding the cake mixture.

Put all the ingredients in a large, roomy bowl and beat well for about 2 minutes, until well blended. Turn the mixture into the tin and smooth the top. Bake in the oven for 35 to 40 minutes, until the cake has shrunk from the sides of the tin and springs back when pressed in the centre with the fingertips.

Leave to cool in the tin, then lift out carefully, still in its foil case, on to a flat surface. Ice as required and cut into pieces.

MAKES 21 pieces

Variations

Fruit Cake   Add 6 to 8 oz (175 to 225 g) currants to the other ingredients in the bowl and sprinkle 1 level tablespoon demerara sugar over the cake half way through the cooking time.

Lemon Cake   Add the grated rind of 1½ lemons to the cake ingredients. When the cake comes out of the oven, mix the juice of 1½ lemons with 6 oz (175 g) caster or granulated sugar and spoon over the hot cake. If the lemons have a lot of juice, the lemon and sugar mixture will be runny; otherwise, it will be more like a sugary paste which has to be spread over the cake with the back of a spoon.

Chocolate Cake   Blend 3 level tablespoons cocoa with 3 tablespoons hot water in the mixing bowl first of all. Add the remaining ingredients and make the cake as above. Leave to cool in the tin. Melt 3 oz (75 g) margarine in a small saucepan, then stir in 2 oz (50 g) sieved cocoa and cook over a gentle heat for 1 minute. Remove from the heat and stir in 8 oz (225 g) sieved icing sugar and 2 tablespoons milk. Beat well until the icing has thickened, then spread over the cake. Leave to set.

Bakewell Open Tart   Line the tin with shortcrust pastry made with 6 oz (175 g) flour and 3 oz (75 g) margarine. Spread the pastry with raspberry jam. Top with the basic cake mixture made up using 2 eggs and 4 oz (100 g) soft margarine, and reducing all the other ingredients by one third too, and add to this ½ teaspoon almond essence. If you like, sprinkle the sponge mixture with flaked almonds.

Black Treacle Cake   Use only 4½ oz (125 g) caster sugar in the basic mixture, then add 7 oz (200 g) black treacle and 1½ level teaspoons mixed spice. The cake looks nice if sprinkled with sieved icing sugar when cooled.

Cherry Tray Bake   Make and bake a basic tray bake sponge. When cool, ice with a vanilla icing made with 3 oz (75 g) soft margarine, 8 oz (225 g) sieved icing sugar, 1 tablespoon milk and vanilla essence to flavour. Spread over the top of the cake, mark into bars and decorate each bar with halved glacé cherries.

Meringues

Make meringues by this foolproof method and I guarantee success. Use non-stick silicone paper, which can be bought from any good stationer and may be brushed off after use and used again and again. I like meringues to be off-white in colour so that they look home-made, not stark white like many of the shop-bought variety. If you like more toffee-flavoured ones, use half caster and half light muscovado sugar. Any meringues that get broken can be used to make Bergen Lemon Cream or Scotch Mist (*page 173*).

PREPARATION AND COOKING TIME: 4 hours

4 egg whites
8 oz (225 g) caster sugar
whipping cream

Heat the oven to 200°F/100°C/Gas Mark ¼ and line two baking sheets with silicone paper.

Place the egg whites in a large bowl and whisk on high speed with an electric or hand rotary whisk until they form soft peaks. Add the sugar, a teaspoonful at a time, whisking well after each addition, until all the sugar has been added. Using two dessertspoons, spoon the meringue out on to the baking sheets, putting 12 meringues on each tray.

Bake in the oven for 3 to 4 hours, until the meringues are firm and dry and will lift easily from the silicone paper. (They will be a very pale off-white, or slightly darker if you have used muscovado sugar.) Whip the cream until it is thick and use it to sandwich the meringues together when they are cool.

MAKES 12 meringues

Swiss Roll

Home-made Swiss roll is not difficult to make if you follow these instructions and if you weigh all the ingredients accurately.

PREPARATION AND COOKING TIME: 30 minutes

3 size 2 eggs, at room temperature
3 oz (75 g) caster sugar, warmed
3 oz (75 g) self-raising flour
caster sugar
about 4 tablespoons raspberry jam

Heat the oven to 425°F/220°C/Gas Mark 7. Grease and line with greased greaseproof paper a 13 by 9 inch (33 by 23 cm) Swiss roll tin.

Whisk the eggs and sugar together in a large bowl until the mixture is light and creamy and the whisk will leave a trail when lifted out. Sieve the flour and carefully fold it into the mixture, using a metal spoon.

Turn the mixture into the tin and give it a gentle shake, or smooth level with the back of the spoon, so that the mixture finds its own level and it is spread evenly into the corners. Bake in the oven for about 10 minutes, until the sponge is golden brown and begins to shrink from the edges of the tin.

While the cake is cooking, cut out a piece of greaseproof paper a little bigger than the tin and sprinkle it with caster sugar. Heat the jam in a small pan until it is of a consistency that is just easy to spread (if it is too hot, the jam will soak into the sponge).

Invert the cake on to the sugared paper. Quickly loosen the paper on the bottom of the cake and peel it off. To make rolling easier, trim all four edges of the sponge and make a score mark 1 inch (2.5 cm) in from one short edge, being careful not to cut right through. Spread the cake with jam, taking it almost to the edges. Fold the narrow strip created by the score mark down on to the jam and begin rolling, using the paper to keep a firm roll.

Leave for a few minutes with the paper still around it, to settle. Lift the Swiss roll on to a wire rack, remove the paper, sprinkle with more sugar and leave to cool completely.

All-in-One Victoria Sandwich

This is very quick and gives excellent results every time – indeed, it is just as good as the old-fashioned creaming method. If you like a deep Victoria sandwich, use two 7 inch (17.5 cm) tins for this amount.

PREPARATION AND COOKING TIME: 40 minutes

6 oz (175 g) soft margarine
6 oz (175 g) caster sugar
3 eggs, beaten
6 oz (175 g) self-raising flour
1½ level teaspoons baking powder
about 6 tablespoons strawberry or raspberry jam
a little caster sugar to decorate

Heat the oven to 350°F/180°C/Gas Mark 4. Grease and line with greased greaseproof paper two 8 inch (20 cm) round sandwich tins.

Measure the margarine, sugar, eggs, flour and baking powder into a large mixing bowl and beat well until thoroughly blended. Divide between the tins, level out evenly and bake in the oven for 25 to 30 minutes, until well risen and the top of the sponges spring back when lightly pressed with a finger.

Leave to cool in the tins for a few minutes then turn out, remove the paper and finish cooling on a cake rack. When completely cold, sandwich the cakes together with the jam. Lift on to a serving plate and serve sprinkled with caster sugar.

Variations

Lemon Sandwich   Add the finely grated rind of 1 lemon to the cake mixture. Sandwich together with lemon curd and ice with lemon glacé icing made with 6 oz (175 g) icing sugar and some lemon juice.

Chocolate Sandwich   Blend 2 rounded tablespoons cocoa with 5 tablespoons hot water in the mixing bowl first of all. Cool, then add the other
ingredients and proceed as above. Fill and top the cake with white butter
cream: blend 3 oz (75 g) soft margarine with 8 oz (225 g) sieved icing sugar.
Decorate with grated chocolate.

Coffee Sandwich   Dissolve 2 heaped teaspoonfuls instant coffee in the
beaten eggs before adding to the mixture. Fill the centre with coffee butter
cream (add 1 tablespoon coffee essence to the white butter cream above) and
dredge the top of the sponge with a little sieved icing sugar.

First-Rate Chocolate Cake

A real Sunday best cake! Large, moist and luxurious, it is very rich so cut thin slices – they can always come back for more. I always spread the cake generously with apricot jam.

PREPARATION AND COOKING TIME: 45 minutes

2 rounded tablespoons cocoa
5 tablespoons very hot water
8 oz (225 g) soft margarine
8 oz (225 g) caster sugar
4 eggs
8 oz (225 g) self-raising flour
2 level teaspoons baking powder
2 oz (50 g) plain chocolate cake covering

ICING AND FILLING
3 oz (75 g) margarine
2 oz (50 g) cocoa
3 tablespoons milk
12 oz (350 g) icing sugar, sieved
apricot jam, warmed

Heat the oven to 350°F/180°C/Gas Mark 4. Grease and line with greased greaseproof paper two 9 inch (23 cm) round sandwich tins.

Blend the cocoa with the hot water in a large bowl. Add the margarine, sugar, eggs, flour and baking powder to the bowl and beat with a wooden spoon for 2 to 3 minutes, or beat using an electric mixer. Turn into the tins and bake in the oven for about 25 minutes. When cooked the cakes will have shrunk slightly from the sides of the tin and will spring back when lightly pressed with a finger. Turn out, remove the paper and leave to cool on wire racks.

Melt the chocolate in a bowl over hot water. Spread it on a marble or laminated plastic surface and leave for a few moments to set. Take a French cook's knife, hold it at a 45° angle and push the chocolate forward in curls. Lift them on to a plate.

To make the icing, melt the margarine in a small saucepan and stir in the cocoa. Cook over a gentle heat for 1 minute, then remove from the heat and add the milk and icing sugar. Beat well to mix, then leave to cool, stirring occasionally, until the icing has thickened to a coating consistency.

Spread one cake with apricot jam, then with a good tablespoon of icing, and place the second cake on top. Spread with apricot jam, covering the sides and top. Pour or spread the remaining icing all over the cake and decorate with the chocolate curls.

Can't-Go-Wrong Chocolate Cake

A moist chocolate cake that really can't go wrong and keeps well.

PREPARATION AND COOKING TIME: 45 minutes

6½ oz (190 g) flour
2 level tablespoons cocoa
1 level teaspoon bicarbonate of soda
1 level teaspoon baking powder
5 oz (150 g) caster sugar
2 tablespoons golden syrup
2 eggs, beaten
¼ pint (150 ml) sunflower oil
¼ pint (150 ml) milk
a little warmed apricot jam
chocolate flake, to decorate

ICING
2 oz (50 g) margarine
1 oz (25 g) cocoa, sieved
about 3 tablespoons milk
8 oz (225 g) icing sugar, sieved

Heat the oven to 325°F/160°C/Gas Mark 3 and grease and line with greased greaseproof paper the bases of two 8 inch (20 cm) straight-sided sandwich tins.

Sift the dry ingredients into a large bowl, and make a well in the centre. Add the syrup, eggs, oil and milk, beat well and pour into the tins. Bake in the oven for 30 to 35 minutes, or until the cake springs back when lightly pressed with the fingertips. Turn out on a wire rack, remove the paper and leave to cool.

For the icing, melt the margarine in a small pan, add the cocoa, stir to blend and cook gently for 1 minute. Stir in the milk and icing sugar, remove from the heat and mix very well, then leave on one side, stirring occasionally until the icing thickens. Spread one cake with apricot jam, then with half the icing, and sandwich the cakes together. Top the cake with more jam and icing, swirling the icing with a knife to give an attractive appearance. Decorate with bits of chocolate flake.

Frosted Walnut Cake

I have happy memories of a Fullers' walnut cake, and this is very similar. The frosting is far simpler than the traditional American variety.

PREPARATION AND COOKING TIME: 1 hour

8 oz (225 g) plain flour
1 oz (25 g) cornflour
3 level teaspoons baking powder
6 oz (175 g) unsalted butter,
  softened
12 oz (350 g) caster sugar
scant 8 fl oz (250 ml) milk
4 egg whites
3 oz (75 g) shelled walnuts,
  chopped
walnut halves to decorate

FROSTING
12 oz (350 g) caster sugar
2 egg whites
4 tablespoons water
½ teaspoon cream of tartar
pinch of salt
few drops vanilla essence

Heat the oven to 350°F/180°C/Gas Mark 4. Grease and line two 8 inch (20 cm) sandwich tins, using a band of greased greaseproof paper with diagonal cuts at the base to make it fit around the tin. (The band should stick up above the top of the tin as the cake will rise a good deal.) Then drop in a circle of greased greaseproof paper a shade smaller than the tin.

Sift the flour, cornflour and baking powder on to a plate. Cream the butter and sugar together until light and fluffy. Stir in the flour and milk alternately, with a folding action, until blended. Whisk the egg whites until stiff, fold into the cake mixture with the nuts and divide between the tins.

Bake for about 35 minutes until well risen. The top of the cake will be springy and the sides shrinking away from the paper. Cool and remove the paper.

To make the frosting, measure the ingredients into a bowl over a pan of simmering water. Stir until the sugar has dissolved, then whisk with an electric hand whisk or balloon whisk until the mixture stands up in peaks. Scrape down the sides of the bowl from time to time.

Sandwich the cakes together with a third of the frosting and then cover with the remainder. Decorate with walnut halves.

Simnel Cake

Now the traditional Easter cake, it was originally given by servant girls to their mothers on Mothering Sunday. Make the glacé icing with 6 oz (175 g) icing sugar, lemon juice to mix and a dash of yellow food colouring. To crystallise primroses, beat a little egg white and brush this over the flowers and their leaves, then dust with caster sugar on both sides. Stand the primroses on a wire cake rack in a warm place until crisp and dry – this takes a few hours.

PREPARATION AND COOKING TIME: 2 hours

6 oz (175 g) soft margarine or
   butter
6 oz (175 g) light soft brown sugar
3 eggs
6 oz (175 g) self-raising flour
2 level teaspoons mixed spice
10 oz (275 g) mixed dried fruit

2 oz (50 g) ground almonds
12 oz (350 g) almond paste
a little pale yellow glacé icing
   (above)
crystallised primroses (above) or
   sugared eggs to decorate

Heat the oven to 325°F/160°C/Gas Mark 3, and grease and line with greaseproof paper an 8 inch (20 cm) round cake tin.

Put the margarine, sugar, eggs, flour, spice, fruit and almonds in a large mixing bowl and beat together with a wooden spoon, until well blended – this will take 2 to 3 minutes.

Place half the cake mixture in the bottom of the tin and smooth the top. Take the almond paste and roll out to a circle the size of the tin, then place on top of the cake mixture. Cover with the remaining cake mixture and smooth the top. Bake in the oven for about 1½ hours, until evenly browned and shrinking away from the edge of the tin. Turn out, remove the paper and leave to cool on a wire rack.

Pour the icing over the centre of the cake, leaving a margin of about 1 inch (2.5 cm). When the icing has set, decorate with crystallised primroses or sugared eggs.

Pineapple Fruit Cake

As this is a very moist cake, it is best kept in the refrigerator and eaten within six weeks. I have known it to go mouldy if left in a cake tin in a warm kitchen.

PREPARATION AND COOKING TIME: 1¾ hours

2 oz (50 g) glacé cherries, halved
7 oz (200 g) self-raising flour
8 oz (225 g) can pineapple pieces, drained
5 oz (150 g) soft margarine
5 oz (150 g) light muscovado sugar
2 eggs, beaten
2 tablespoons milk
12 oz (350 g) mixed dried fruit

Heat the oven to 325°F/160°C/Gas Mark 3. Grease and line with greased greaseproof paper an 8 inch (20 cm) round cake tin. Roll the cherries in a little of the flour and finely chop the drained pineapple.

In a bowl, cream the margarine and sugar, then gradually beat in the eggs. Gently fold in the remaining flour, milk, dried fruit, cherries and pineapple.

Turn into the prepared tin, smooth the top and bake in the oven for about 1½ hours, until the cake is a pale golden brown and shrinking from the sides of the tin. Leave in the tin until quite cold before turning out. Store in the refrigerator.

Special Apricot Cake

Utterly delicious. A can of apricots is added to this cake and gives it its distinctive flavour. Use the juice from the can in a fruit salad or soak sponge cakes in it for a trifle.

PREPARATION AND COOKING TIME: 1¾ hours

4 oz (100 g) soft margarine
4 oz (100 g) soft light brown sugar
2 large eggs
¼ teaspoon almond essence
7 oz (200 g) self-raising flour
½ level teaspoon baking powder
7½ oz (210 g) can apricot halves, drained and chopped
8 oz (225 g) mixed dried fruit

Heat the oven to 325°F/160°C/Gas Mark 3 and grease and line with greased greaseproof paper a 7 inch (17.5 cm) cake tin.

Cream the margarine and sugar until light and creamy. Beat in the eggs and almond essence, adding a tablespoon of flour with the last of the egg. Fold in the remaining flour, baking powder, apricots and dried fruit.

Turn the mixture into the tin, smooth the top and bake in the oven for 1½ hours, or until the cake is golden brown and a skewer inserted in the centre comes out clean. Cool in the tin for 10 minutes, then turn out, remove the paper, and leave to cool completely on a wire rack.

Mincemeat Fruit Loaves

Many moons ago I invented the mincemeat cake, and over the years I have varied the ingredients slightly. This version is made in 1 lb (450 g) loaf tins, as on more than one occasion W.I. members have told me how useful it is to sell on W.I. markets. You can, of course, double up this recipe and bake four at a time – much easier to fit in the oven than round tins! But do remember that the more you fill the oven, the longer the loaves will take to cook. The exception is if you have a fan oven.

PREPARATION AND COOKING TIME: 1¼ hours

2 eggs
5 oz (150 g) caster sugar
5 oz (150 g) soft margarine
8 oz (225 g) self-raising flour
12 oz (350 g) mincemeat
8 oz (225 g) currants
a few flaked almonds

Heat the oven to 325°F/160°C/Gas Mark 3. Grease and line with greased greaseproof paper two 1 lb (450 g) loaf tins.

Crack the eggs into a large, roomy bowl and add all the other ingredients except the flaked almonds. Mix well until blended, then divide the mixture between the two tins and level out evenly. Sprinkle with flaked almonds.

Bake in the oven for about 1¼ hours, until risen, pale golden brown and shrinking away from the sides of the tin. A fine skewer inserted in the centre of the loaves should come out clean. Turn out of the tins and cool on a wire rack. Peel off the paper and store in an airtight tin.

MAKES 2 loaves

Cherry Cake

A classic cake. It is important to cut the cherries up and then wash and dry them thoroughly so that all moisture is removed.

PREPARATION AND COOKING TIME: 1½ hours

6 oz (175 g) glacé cherries
8 oz (225 g) self-raising flour
6 oz (175 g) soft butter or margarine
6 oz (175 g) caster sugar
finely grated rind of 1 lemon
2 oz (50 g) ground almonds
3 large eggs

Heat the oven to 350°F/180°C/Gas Mark 4 and grease and line with greased greaseproof paper a 7 inch (17.5 cm) round cake tin.

Cut each cherry into quarters, and rinse in a sieve under running water. Drain well and dry very thoroughly on absorbent kitchen paper.

Place all the remaining ingredients in a large bowl and beat well for 1 minute, then lightly fold in the cherries. The mixture will be fairly stiff, which will help to keep the cherries evenly suspended in the cake while it is baking.

Turn into the prepared tin and bake in the oven for about 1¼ hours, or until a warm skewer inserted in the centre comes out clean. Leave to cool in the tin for 10 minutes then turn out and finish cooling on a wire rack. Store in an airtight tin.

Madeira Cake

I always used to make this with butter but I find soft margarines give a really well-flavoured result.

PREPARATION AND COOKING TIME: 1¾ hours

8 oz (225 g) self-raising flour
6 oz (175 g) soft margarine
7 oz (200 g) caster sugar
4 eggs
finely grated rind of 1 lemon
piece of lemon citron peel, washed and dried

Heat the oven to 350°F/180°C/Gas Mark 4. Grease and line with greased greaseproof paper a 7 inch (17 cm) round cake tin.

Measure all the ingredients except the peel into a bowl and beat well until smooth. Spread the mixture in the prepared tin and level the surface.

Bake for 30 minutes, until set, then carefully place the peel on the centre of the cake. Reduce the oven temperature to 325°F/160°C/Gas Mark 3 and cook for a further hour. The cake should be shrinking away slightly from the sides of the tin and be pale golden in colour.

Cool in the tin for about 10 minutes, then turn out, peel off the paper and finish cooling on a wire rack.

Butter Almond Cake

A lovely light cake, perfect for coffee mornings. Well worth trying.

PREPARATION AND COOKING TIME: 1½ hours

6 oz (175 g) butter, softened
6 oz (175 g) caster sugar
4 eggs, beaten
4 oz (100 g) ground almonds
7 oz (200 g) self-raising flour
1 teaspoon almond essence
1 oz (25 g) flaked almonds

Heat the oven to 350°F/180°C/Gas Mark 4. Grease and line with greased greaseproof paper an 8 inch (20 cm) deep round cake tin.

Measure the butter and sugar into a bowl and beat well until light and fluffy. Beat in the eggs a little at a time. Gently fold in the ground almonds, flour and almond essence until thoroughly blended. Turn into the prepared tin and level out evenly.

Bake in the oven for about 1¼ hours, until well risen and golden brown. A skewer should come out clean when inserted in the centre of the cake. Leave to cool in the tin for a few minutes, then turn out, peel off the paper and finish cooling on a wire rack.

Superb Carrot Cake

America has gone mad on carrot cakes. This is gooey and delicious.

PREPARATION AND COOKING TIME: 1½ hours

8 oz (225 g) self-raising flour
2 level teaspoons baking powder
5 oz (150 g) light soft brown sugar
2 oz (50 g) shelled walnuts, chopped
4 oz (100 g) carrots, washed, trimmed and grated
2 ripe bananas, mashed
2 eggs
¼ pint (150 ml) sunflower oil

TOPPING
3 oz (75 g) soft margarine
3 oz (75 g) cream cheese
6 oz (175 g) icing sugar, sieved
½ teaspoon vanilla essence

Heat the oven to 350°F/180°C/Gas Mark 4. Grease and line an 8 inch (20 cm) round cake tin with a circle of greased greaseproof paper.

Measure the flour and baking powder into a large bowl and stir in the sugar. Add the nuts, carrots and bananas, and mix lightly. Make a well in the centre, add the eggs and oil, and beat well until blended.

Turn into the tin and bake in the oven for about 1¼ hours, until the cake is golden brown and is shrinking slightly from the sides of the tin. A warm skewer inserted in the centre should come out clean. Turn out, remove the paper, and leave to cool on a wire rack.

Place all the ingredients for the topping in a bowl, and beat well until blended and smooth. Spread over the cake and rough up the surface with a fork. Leave in a cool place for the icing to harden slightly before serving.

Wholemeal Orange Cake

For a less rich cake, simply sandwich together with 3 tablespoons lemon curd blended with 3 tablespoons natural yoghurt.

PREPARATION AND COOKING TIME: 45 minutes

6 oz (175 g) margarine
6 oz (175 g) light muscovado sugar
3 eggs
6 oz (175 g) self-raising wholemeal flour
1 level teaspoon baking powder
grated rind of 1 orange
2 tablespoons milk

FILLING AND TOPPING
3 oz (75 g) margarine
8 oz (225 g) icing sugar, sieved
3 tablespoons orange juice

Heat the oven to 350°F/180°C/Gas Mark 4. Grease two 8 inch (20 cm) sandwich tins.

Measure all the ingredients for the cake into a bowl and beat well for about 2 minutes, until blended and smooth. Divide the mixture between the two tins and level the tops.

Bake in the oven for 25 to 30 minutes. When cooked, the cakes will have shrunk away from the sides of the tins and will spring back when lightly pressed with a finger. Turn the sponges out on to a wire rack and allow to cool.

For the filling and topping, measure all the ingredients into a bowl and blend together until smooth. Use half to sandwich the cakes together and spread the remainder on top, then mark decoratively with a fork and allow to set.

Teabreads, Biscuits and Scones

The most practical shape for teabreads is the loaf shape. If you are not a big family, make two small loaves and freeze one.

All the things in this chapter are excellent for adding to a packed lunch, and home-made biscuits cannot be matched by anything out of a packet. Scones, so quick and inexpensive to make, are the perfect solution when unexpected visitors arrive at teatime.

Orange Teabread

A simple teabread with a lovely orange flavour. Prepare the fruit one afternoon with leftover tea, leave to stand overnight, then make the bread the next morning. This teabread is good on its own or spread with butter.

PREPARATION AND COOKING TIME: 1¾ hours

5 oz (150 g) currants
5 oz (150 g) raisins
5 oz (150 g) light soft brown sugar
finely grated rind of 2 oranges
½ pint (300 ml) hot tea
10 oz (275 g) self-raising flour
1 egg

Put the fruit, sugar and orange rind in a bowl and pour on the tea. Stir very well, cover with a plate to keep in the heat, and leave to stand overnight.

Next day, heat the oven to 300°F/150°C/Gas Mark 2 and grease and line with greased greaseproof paper an 8 inch (20 cm) round cake tin.

Stir the flour into the soaked fruit and mix very well. Turn the mixture into the prepared tin and bake in the oven for about 1½ hours, or until the bread has shrunk from the sides of the tin and a warm skewer inserted in the centre comes out clean. Turn out, remove the paper and leave to cool on a wire rack.

Fruit Malt Loaf

This loaf is so easy (and so good) that I am sure children could make it. All the ingredients are likely to be to hand in the store cupboard.

PREPARATION AND COOKING TIME: 1 hour

6 oz (175 g) self-raising flour
2 tablespoons malt drink (Ovaltine)
1 oz (25 g) caster or soft light brown sugar
3 oz (75 g) sultanas
2 tablespoons golden syrup
¼ pint (150 ml) milk

Heat the oven to 350°F/180°C/Gas Mark 4 and well grease a 1 lb (450 g) loaf tin.

Put all the ingredients in a large bowl and mix together until a thick batter is formed. Turn the mixture into the tin and then bake in the oven for 50 to 60 minutes, or until a skewer inserted in the centre comes out clean. Turn out and leave to cool on a wire rack.

Fruity Gingerbread

Gingerbread always tastes better if you keep it, stored in an airtight tin, for 2 or 3 days before eating.

PREPARATION AND COOKING TIME: 1½ hours

1 level teaspoon mixed spice
2 level teaspoons ground ginger
1 level teaspoon bicarbonate of soda
8 oz (225 g) plain flour
3 oz (75 g) soft margarine
4 oz (100 g) black treacle
4 oz (100 g) golden syrup
2 oz (50 g) dark soft brown sugar
2 oz (50 g) chunky marmalade, roughly chopped
2 eggs, beaten
6 tablespoons milk
4 oz (100 g) mixed dried fruit

Heat the oven to 325°F/160°C/Gas Mark 3. Grease and line with greased greaseproof paper an 8 inch (20 cm) square tin.

Sift the spices, bicarbonate of soda and flour into a bowl and make a well in the centre.

Place the margarine in a saucepan, together with the treacle, syrup and sugar, and heat until the margarine has just melted and the ingredients have blended. Draw the pan from the heat and leave to cool slightly. Stir the marmalade, eggs, milk and fruit into the bowl of flour, together with the margarine mixture, and beat with a wooden spoon until smooth and glossy. Pour into the tin and bake in the oven for 1 to 1¼ hours.

Leave the gingerbread to cool in the tin for about 30 minutes before turning it out and removing the paper. Leave it on a wire rack until it is completely cool. Store in an airtight tin.

RIGHT: *Welsh Cakes (page 226), Orange Teabread (page 222) and Fruit Malt Loaf (page 223)*

Banana Loaf

A delicious cut-and-come-again loaf that really tastes of banana. Serve in slices, on its own or spread with butter.

PREPARATION AND COOKING TIME: 1¾ hours

2 ripe bananas, mashed with a fork
4 oz (100 g) wholemeal flour
5 oz (150 g) self-raising flour
2 level teaspoons baking powder
4 oz (100 g) soft margarine
6 oz (175 g) light muscovado sugar
2 large eggs, beaten
¼ pint (150 ml) natural yoghurt
5 oz (150 g) currants
2 tablespoons milk

Heat the oven to 350°F/180°C/Gas Mark 4. Grease and line with greased greaseproof paper a 2 lb (900 g) loaf tin.

Measure all the ingredients into a large mixing bowl and beat well until thoroughly blended. Turn into the prepared tin and bake in the oven for about 1½ hours, until well risen. Test the loaf with a warm fine skewer: if the skewer comes out clean, the loaf is done.

Leave the banana loaf to cool in the tin for about 15 minutes, then turn out, remove the paper, and finish cooling on a cake rack.

LEFT: *Asparagus Rolls (page 243), Cashew Nutters (page 247), Melon and Parma Ham (page 242) and Cheese Filo Puffs (page 246)*

Welsh Cakes

These are very quick to prepare and may be made on a traditional griddle or in a heavy non-stick frying pan. Do not cook the cakes too fast, otherwise the centres will not be fully cooked through. They are best eaten on the day that they are made.

PREPARATION AND COOKING TIME: 20 minutes

8 oz (225 g) self-raising flour
4 oz (100 g) margarine
3 oz (75 g) caster sugar
3 oz (75 g) currants
½ level teaspoon mixed spice
1 egg
1 to 2 tablespoons milk
icing sugar

Put the flour in a bowl and rub in the margarine until the mixture resembles fine breadcrumbs. Add the sugar, currants and spice. Beat the egg with the milk, add this to the flour and mix to a firm dough. Roll out the dough to about ¼ inch (5 mm) thickness and cut into rounds with a plain 3 inch (7.5 cm) cutter.

Heat and lightly grease a griddle or heavy frying pan. Cook the Welsh cakes on a low heat for about 3 minutes on each side until golden brown, then leave to cool on a wire rack. Dust with icing sugar before serving.

MAKES 12 to 14 Welsh cakes

Brioches

Serve these in place of bread rolls with a special dinner. They also make a delicious breakfast with butter and marmalade – if possible, serve warm. I find it easiest to use the type of dried yeast you add directly to the flour.

PREPARATION AND COOKING TIME: 30 minutes
PROVING TIME: 1¾ hours

9 oz (250 g) strong plain white flour
1 oz (25 g) caster sugar
2 oz (50 g) butter
½ oz (15 g) easy-blend dried yeast
3 tablespoons hand-hot milk
2 eggs, beaten
a little beaten egg to glaze

Measure the flour and sugar into a large mixing bowl and rub in the butter until the mixture resembles fine breadcrumbs. Stir in the yeast until thoroughly mixed, then add the milk and eggs and bind together to form a soft dough. Knead until smooth in the bowl, then turn out on to a floured surface and knead well for about 5 minutes. Return to the bowl, cover with clingfilm and leave in a warm place for about an hour, until the dough has doubled in size.

Lightly grease 12 fluted brioche moulds or deep fluted patty tins. Knead the dough again on a floured surface for about 3 minutes, then divide it into 12 equal-sized pieces. Cut a quarter off each piece, form the larger part into a bowl and place in a mould. Press a hole firmly into the centre of the ball and place the remaining small piece of dough as a knob on top of this. When all the brioches are formed, cover with a piece of clingfilm and allow to prove for about 45 minutes, until light and puffy.

Heat the oven to 450°F/230°C/Gas Mark 8. Glaze the brioches with beaten egg and bake in the oven for about 12 minutes, until golden brown. Lift out of the moulds and transfer to a cake rack.

MAKES 12 brioches

Lemon Shortbread

This really is one of my favourite shortbreads. It keeps extremely well in an airtight tin and is delicious to serve with a cup of coffee.

PREPARATION AND COOKING TIME: 45 minutes

4 oz (100 g) butter, softened
2 oz (50 g) caster sugar
4 oz (100 g) flour
2 oz (50 g) cornflour
grated rind of 1 large lemon
caster sugar for topping

Heat the oven to 325°F/160°C/Gas Mark 3, and lightly grease a 7 inch (17.5 cm) square tin.

Cream the butter and sugar together in a mixing bowl until light, then work in the flours and lemon rind. Knead well until smooth. Press the mixture into the prepared tin, level the top and bake in the oven for about 35 minutes, or until a pale golden brown.

Remove from the oven and mark into fingers, then leave in the tin to become quite cold before lifting out with a metal spatula on to a cake rack. Sprinkle with caster sugar before serving.

MAKES 12 fingers

Chocolate Caramel Shortbread

These are great favourites with all ages. Don't expect the caramel to harden – it does not – and the shortbread is gooey and sticky to eat.

PREPARATION AND COOKING TIME: 45 minutes

4 oz (100 g) soft margarine
2 oz (50 g) caster sugar
6 oz (175 g) plain flour
4 oz (100 g) plain chocolate

CARAMEL
4 oz (100 g) margarine
3 oz (75 g) caster sugar
2 level tablespoons golden syrup
6 oz (175 g) can condensed milk

Heat the oven to 350°F/180°C/Gas Mark 4. Grease a 7 by 11 inch (17.5 by 28 cm) Swiss roll tin.

Place the margarine, sugar and flour for the shortbread in a bowl and beat to a firm dough. (The mixture may require a light kneading with the hand to come together.) Press into the tin with the back of a metal spoon or the palm of the hand, then prick with a fork and bake for 25 to 30 minutes until a pale brown.

While the shortbread is baking, prepare the caramel. Put all the ingredients in a saucepan and heat gently until melted, then boil the mixture for 5 to 10 minutes until caramel coloured. Stir continuously, preferably with a flat-based wooden spoon which can get into the sides of the pan and prevent the mixture from catching. Leave to cool slightly. When the shortbread is cooked and has cooled for about 5 minutes, pour the caramel over it and leave on one side.

Break the chocolate into pieces and place in a small bowl over a saucepan of water. Heat gently until the chocolate has melted and is smooth. Pour the chocolate in a steady stream over the caramel and lightly make a swirling pattern with a fork. Leave undisturbed for several hours, then cut into fingers.

MAKES 21 fingers

Florentines

Quite tricky to catch at the right moment before they overcook, so give yourself plenty of time to watch them. I usually have to make a double quantity of these very special biscuits – they disappear so quickly.

PREPARATION AND COOKING TIME: 35 minutes

2 oz (50 g) butter
2 oz (50 g) demerara sugar
2 oz (50 g) golden syrup
2 oz (50 g) flour
4 glacé cherries, finely chopped

2 oz (50 g) currants
2 oz (50 g) chopped nuts such as
  almonds and walnuts
6 oz (175 g) plain chocolate, melted

Heat the oven to 350°F/180°C/Gas Mark 4. Grease two or three large baking sheets.

Measure the butter, sugar and golden syrup into a small pan and heat gently until the butter has melted. Measure the flour, cherries, currants and nuts into a bowl, pour over the melted mixture and stir well until thoroughly combined. Spoon teaspoonfuls of the mixture on to the baking sheets, leaving plenty of space for them to spread, and bake in the oven for 8 to 10 minutes, until golden brown. If you can't bake them all at once, do a few at a time until all the mixture has been used.

Allow to cool for a few moments, then carefully lift them off the baking sheets with a metal spatula, on to a cake rack. Don't let the florentines become too cool, or they will be difficult to lift off the baking sheets. If they do, put them back in the oven for a minute or so to warm through again.

When cold, spread a little melted chocolate over the flat base of each florentine, mark a zigzag in the chocolate with a fork and leave to set, chocolate side up, on the cooling rack. Store in an airtight tin.

MAKES about 20 florentines

Special Scones

If you like brown scones, use wholemeal self-raising flour instead of white self-raising flour. You will find that you need a little more milk. The secret of good scones is not to have the mixture too dry – it should feel a bit sticky. Don't handle the dough too much; cut out quickly and bake. Wrap the scones in a tea towel after baking to keep them moist.

PREPARATION AND COOKING TIME: 20 minutes

8 oz (225 g) self-raising flour
1 teaspoon baking powder
2 oz (50 g) butter, softened
1 oz (25 g) caster sugar
1 egg
about 4 fl oz (120 ml) milk

Heat the oven to 425°F/220°C/Gas Mark 7 and lightly grease a baking sheet.

Sift the flour and salt into a bowl, add the butter and rub in with the fingertips until the mixture resembles fine breadcrumbs. Stir in the sugar.

Crack the egg into a measure and beat lightly, then make up to ¼ pint (150 ml) with milk. Stir into the flour and mix to a soft dough with a little more milk, if necessary. Turn on to a lightly floured table, knead gently and roll out to ½ inch (1.25 cm) thick. Cut into rounds with a 2 inch (5 cm) fluted cutter.

Place the scones on the baking sheet so that they touch, brush the tops with a little milk and bake for 10 minutes, or until pale golden brown. Remove from the baking sheet and leave to cool on a wire tray.

MAKES 10 to 12 scones

Drop Scones

These are simple to make and a great standby when unexpected visitors pop in at the weekend. Serve warm, with butter.

PREPARATION AND COOKING TIME: 15 minutes

4 oz (100 g) self-raising flour
1 oz (25 g) caster sugar
1 egg
¼ pint (150 ml) milk

Prepare a heavy frying pan or the solid plate of an electric cooker. Use a pad of kitchen paper to rub the surface with salt, then grease lightly with lard. When ready to cook the drop scones, heat the pan or hot plate until the lard is just hazy, then wipe off any surplus with more kitchen paper.

Put the flour and sugar in a bowl, make a well in the centre, then add the egg and half the milk and beat to a smooth, thick batter. Beat in the remaining milk.

Spoon the mixture on to the heated surface in spoonfuls, spacing them well. When the bubbles rise to the surface, turn the scones over with a palette knife and cook them on the other side for a further 30 seconds to 1 minute, until golden brown. Lift off on to a wire rack and cover them with a clean tea towel to keep them soft.

Continue cooking until all the batter has been used, then serve at once.

MAKES about 18 drop scones

CHRISTMAS

I have had other birds at Christmas instead of turkey, but turkey remains the favourite. It's also a good buy because there's always plenty left over for eating cold.

I rarely vary the main Christmas meal. It's easier to be organised if you have all your information in one place, so I have included all you need to know in this chapter.

If you are a crowd, you could always have goose or a joint of beef on one of the other days – Christmas seems to go on for about a week now!

Roast Turkey

Thaw the turkey if frozen. Check the weight of the bird with stuffing and calculate the cooking time. Heat the oven.

Put a large piece of foil in the roasting tin, lift the turkey on to it and season well. Wrap the foil over the bird loosely, with the fold at the top, and place on a shelf just below the middle of the oven.

To brown the turkey, undo the foil and rub the breast and legs with butter. Cook with the foil open for the last 1¼ hours of the cooking time for a large bird and about the last 50 minutes for a small bird. The turkey is cooked if when the thickest part of the leg is pierced with a skewer the juices that run out are clear.

After cooking, cover the turkey with foil and keep warm in the oven. Allow to rest for 10 minutes before carving.

ROASTING TIMES

5 lb (2.3 kg)	350°F/180°C/Gas Mark 4	about 2 hours
10 lb (4.5 kg)	350°F/180°C/Gas Mark 4	about 2½ hours
15 lb (6.8 kg)	350°F/180°C/Gas Mark 4	about 3½ hours
20 lb (9 kg)	325°F/160°C/Gas Mark 3	about 4 hours

Trimmings

Chipolata Sausages   Grill the sausages, pricking them if you like, under a medium grill for 10 to 15 minutes. Turn regularly so that they are evenly browned. If you prefer little sausages, give each chipolata a twist in the centre to make it half the size, then cut in two.

Bacon Rolls   Take the rind off streaky bacon rashers and stretch them on a wooden board with the back of a knife so that they are twice their original length. Cut each rasher in half and roll up. Place the bacon rolls on long skewers and grill for 6 minutes under a moderate grill, turning once, so that they are golden brown.

Roast Potatoes   Roast for 1½ to 1¾ hours above the turkey. (They take longer than usual as the oven temperature is lower.) If oven space is short, you could do these in an electric frying pan or even in a deep-fat fryer.

Lemon and Thyme Stuffing

Use to stuff a 14 to 16 lb (6.3 to 7.2 kg) turkey.

1 oz (25 g) butter
1 onion, chopped
1 lb (450 g) pork sausagemeat
4 oz (100 g) fresh white breadcrumbs
grated rind and juice of 1 lemon
salt
freshly ground black pepper
2 tablespoons chopped parsley
1 level teaspoon chopped fresh thyme, or 1 level teaspoon dried thyme

Melt the butter in a saucepan, add the onion and fry gently for about 10 minutes, until soft. Stir in the remaining ingredients and mix well together.

Chestnut Stuffing

Use to stuff a 14 to 16 lb (6.3 to 7.2 kg) turkey. If you cannot get dried chestnuts, use a 1 lb 15 oz (880 g) can of whole chestnuts in water, or 1 lb (450 g) fresh or frozen chestnuts.

8 oz (225 g) dried chestnuts, soaked overnight in cold water
8 oz (225 g) streaky bacon, chopped
2 oz (50 g) butter
4 oz (100 g) fresh breadcrumbs
1 egg, beaten
1 bunch watercress, finely chopped
salt
freshly ground black pepper

Drain the liquid from the chestnuts and chop them coarsely. Fry the bacon slowly to allow the fat to run out, add the chestnuts, then increase the heat and fry quickly until the bacon is crisp and the nuts beginning to colour. Lift out with a slotted spoon and put in a bowl.

Add the butter to the pan with the bacon fat and allow to melt, then add the breadcrumbs and fry until brown. Turn into the bowl, add the remaining ingredients and mix well.

Bread Sauce

3 cloves
1 onion, peeled
¾ pint (450 ml) milk
about 3 oz (75 g) fresh white breadcrumbs
salt
freshly ground black pepper
knob of butter

Stick the cloves in the onion and place it in a saucepan with the milk. Bring slowly to the boil, then turn off the heat and leave the milk to infuse for 30 minutes.

Lift out the onion and stir in the breadcrumbs, seasoning and butter. Reheat almost to boiling point, then remove from the heat. Cover with a piece of damp greaseproof paper and keep warm until required.

Fresh Cranberry Sauce

8 oz (225 g) cranberries
8 oz (225 g) caster sugar
1 thin-skinned orange, quartered and pips removed

Place all the ingredients in a processor or blender and purée to a chunky mince consistency. Turn into a small bowl to serve.

Byre Farm Christmas Pudding

A rich dark special Christmas pudding, the best I have tasted – the recipe has been in my sister-in-law's family for years. It needs only an hour's simmering on Christmas Day.

ADVANCE PREPARATION AND COOKING TIME: 8¼ hours
COOKING TIME ON CHRISTMAS DAY: 1 hour

6 oz (175 g) raisins
3 oz (75 g) currants
3 oz (75 g) sultanas
2 oz (50 g) candied peel, chopped
2 oz (50 g) shelled mixed nuts, chopped
3 oz (75 g) self-raising flour
2 eggs
4 oz (100 g) fresh white breadcrumbs
4 oz (100 g) shredded suet
½ pint (300 ml) stout
1 cooking apple, peeled, cored and diced
grated rind and juice of 1 orange
grated rind and juice of 1 lemon
2 tablespoons black treacle
½ teaspoon nutmeg
½ teaspoon mixed spice

Place all the ingredients in a large bowl and mix together very thoroughly. Turn into a greased 2 pint (1.2 litre) pudding basin, cover with greased greaseproof paper and a foil lid, and simmer in a pan of boiling water for 8 hours. Remove from the pan, cool and cover with a fresh piece of foil to store.

On Christmas Day, cover with clean foil and simmer for 1 hour, then turn out and serve hot with Brandy Butter or Brandy Cream (*page 238*).

SERVES 10 to 12

Brandy Butter

If made in advance, leave the butter at room temperature for about 30 minutes before serving. Store any left over in the freezer for up to 3 months.

8 oz (225 g) unsalted butter
8 oz (225 g) icing sugar, sieved
6 tablespoons brandy

Cream the butter with a wooden spoon until soft, then gradually beat in the icing sugar. Continue beating until the mixture is light and fluffy, then beat in the brandy.

Turn the butter into a serving dish and chill in the refrigerator to harden before serving.

Brandy Cream

Try this for a change as a lighter accompaniment to mince pies and Christmas pudding.

¼ pint (150 ml) double cream
1 tablespoon caster sugar
2 tablespoons brandy

Put all the ingredients in a bowl and whisk until the mixture is thick and forms soft peaks. Pile into a dish and serve chilled.

Mince Pie

One large pie means that you have lots of filling, and I like to make it with a fairly thin lower crust. A generous amount of pastry is included in the recipe, so use the trimmings to make some small pies too. Serve with Brandy Butter or Brandy Cream (*opposite page*).

PREPARATION AND COOKING TIME: 50 minutes
CHILLING TIME: 40 minutes

8 oz (225 g) strong plain flour
6 oz (175 g) hard margarine
scant ¼ pint (150 ml) cold water

FILLING
1 lb (450 g) mincemeat
milk
caster sugar

For the pastry, sift the flour into a mixing bowl. Coarsely grate the margarine into the bowl. Stir in just sufficient water to make a firm dough, then roll out on a lightly floured surface to make a strip about ½ inch (1.25 cm) thick and 6 inches (15 cm) wide. Fold the pastry in three and give it a quarter turn to the left. Roll out again into a strip and fold into three. Wrap the pastry in foil and chill in the refrigerator for 30 minutes.

Divide the pastry into two portions, one slightly larger than the other. Roll out the smaller portion to a circle about ¼ inch (5 mm) thick and use to line a 10 inch (25 cm) enamel, tin or foil pie plate. Spoon in the mincemeat.

Roll out the remaining pastry to a circle ¼ inch (5 mm) thick. Brush the edges of the pie with milk and cover the mincemeat with the second pastry circle. Press the edges firmly together to seal, trim off any excess pastry and crimp the edges to make a decorative finish. Chill for 10 minutes.

Brush the top of the pie with milk and bake in the oven at 425°F/220°C/Gas Mark 7 for 25 minutes, until the pastry is golden brown. Sprinkle with caster sugar and serve warm.

SERVES 8

Victoriana Christmas Cake

An easy, different and special Christmas cake. The dried fruit is soaked for several days in sherry, which makes it very moist. This is not a really deep cake so do not expect it to rise to the top of the tin.

PREPARATION AND COOKING TIME: 3½ hours
SOAKING TIME: at least 3 days

*1¼ lb (550 g) mixed dried fruit,
   including peel*
4 oz (100 g) raisins, chopped
4 oz (100 g) currants
*4 oz (100 g) glacé cherries,
   quartered*
*¼ pint (150 ml) medium or sweet
   sherry*
6 oz (175 g) soft margarine
6 oz (175 g) dark soft brown sugar

grated rind of 1 lemon
grated rind of 1 orange
3 eggs
1 tablespoon black treacle
*2 oz (50 g) blanched almonds,
   chopped*
4 oz (100 g) plain flour
2 oz (50 g) self-raising flour
1 level teaspoon mixed spice

Put the fruit and cherries in a container, pour over the sherry, cover with a lid and leave to soak for at least 3 days, stirring daily.

Put the margarine, sugar, lemon and orange rind, eggs, treacle and almonds in a large bowl. Sift together the flours and spice and add to the bowl. Mix together until evenly blended, then stir in the soaked fruit and sherry.

Heat the oven to 300°F/150°C/Gas Mark 2 and grease and line with greased greaseproof paper an 8 inch (20 cm) round cake tin. Spoon in the mixture and smooth the top flat. Bake in the oven for 2 hours, then reduce the heat to 275°F/140°C/Gas Mark 1 and bake for a further 1¼ hours. (If the cake seems to be getting too brown on top, cover it very loosely with a sheet of foil).

Test with a warm skewer to see if the cake is done. If the skewer comes out clean when inserted in the centre of the cake, it is cooked. If not, bake for a further 15 minutes. Leave to cool in the tin.

FOOD TO
GO WITH DRINKS

My two golden rules are don't offer too much of a variety, and use smallish trays that are constantly refilled. Serve some of everything on each tray and keep the presentation simple.

Always choose some things that can be prepared well ahead and possibly frozen, and give everyone a drink before you bring in the food. And don't leave half-empty trays sitting around afterwards!

Melon and Parma Ham

Parma ham can now be bought in vacuum packs from most good super-markets. When buying the melon, choose whatever variety is the best for the time of year.

PREPARATION TIME: 15 minutes
CHILLING TIME: 1 hour

1 small ripe melon
6 long thin slices Parma ham
juice of ½ lemon
freshly ground black pepper
lemon wedges to garnish

Cut the melon into eight wedges. Scoop out and discard the seeds from each slice and cut off the skin. Divide the wedges into bite-sized pieces. Cut the slices of ham into about 30 little strips (one for each chunk of melon). Roll a strip of ham around each chunk of melon, and spear with a cocktail stick to make for easier eating.

Arrange the melon on a platter and squeeze the lemon juice over it. Season with a little black pepper and decorate with lemon wedges. Serve well chilled.

MAKES about 30 pieces

Asparagus Rolls

Use a Hovis loaf when making asparagus rolls as this is the easiest bread to roll without it all crumbling and breaking up.

PREPARATION TIME: 15 minutes

1 lb (450 g) frozen asparagus spears, thawed
1 small Hovis loaf
4 oz (100 g) butter, softened

Blanch the asparagus in a pan of boiling salted water for a minute, then refresh under running cold water and drain well on kitchen paper. Cut the crusts off the loaf so that the loaf measures 2½ inches (6 cm) square, then carefully cut the loaf into slices with a very sharp bread knife. Butter the slices of bread and lay a spear of asparagus diagonally across each piece from corner to corner.

Carefully roll up the bread so there is a V-shape on top of the roll. Arrange on a serving dish, cover with clingfilm and store in the refrigerator until required.

MAKES about 36 rolls

Bacon and Liver Kebabs

These tiny kebabs can be prepared well in advance and refrigerated, then arranged on a serving dish and reheated in the oven as required.

PREPARATION AND COOKING TIME: 40 minutes

8 oz (225 g) chicken livers
2 oz (50 g) seasoned flour
sunflower oil for frying
about 6 rashers streaky bacon, cut in half

Rinse any blood from the livers, dry on kitchen paper then toss in the seasoned flour until evenly coated. Heat the oil in a pan and quickly fry the livers for about 2 minutes, until just tender. Remove from the heat, drain well on kitchen paper, and cut each in half.

Wrap each piece of liver in bacon, pierce with a wooden cocktail stick and cook under a hot grill until the bacon is crisp. Allow to cool, then arrange on a heatproof serving dish ready to heat through when required.

To serve, cook in the oven at 350°F/180°C/Gas Mark 4 for about 25 minutes, until warmed through.

MAKES about 12 kebabs

Cheese Aigrettes

These little savoury choux pastry balls are good to serve as a snack with drinks. Alternatively, serve with coffee at the end of a meal in place of mint chocolates. When I had a Victorian buffet party to celebrate my birthday, I served them right at the end of the meal as a course in their own right.

PREPARATION AND COOKING TIME: 40 minutes

2 oz (50 g) butter
½ pint (300 ml) water
4 oz (100 g) self-raising flour
2 egg yolks
2 eggs
4 oz (100 g) well-flavoured Cheddar cheese, grated
salt
freshly ground black pepper
oil for deep-frying

Put the butter and water in a small pan and bring to the boil. Remove from the heat and add the flour all at once. Beat well until the mixture is smooth and glossy and leaves the sides of the pan clean. Cool slightly.

Lightly mix the yolks and eggs together and beat into the mixture a little at a time. Stir in the cheese and seasoning. Drop the mixture in teaspoonfuls into hot deep fat and fry gently until golden brown. Lift out and drain on kitchen paper. Serve warm.

To reheat the aigrettes for a party, arrange them on a baking sheet and heat in the oven at 425°F/220°C/Gas Mark 7 for about 12 minutes, until heated through and crispy.

MAKES about 36 aigrettes

Cheese Filo Puffs

Filo pastry or paste – also spelt *fillo* or *phyllo* – is available in sheets from delicatessens, continental grocers and some good supermarkets. It freezes well. Prepare these puffs in advance and bake as needed.

PREPARATION AND COOKING TIME: 30 minutes

1 lb (450 g) packet of filo pastry
6 oz (175 g) unsalted butter, melted

FILLING
2 oz (50 g) butter
2 oz (50 g) flour
½ pint (300 ml) milk
salt
freshly ground black pepper
freshly grated nutmeg
1 teaspoon Dijon mustard
8 oz (225 g) well-flavoured Cheddar cheese, grated

Heat the oven to 400°F/200°C/Gas Mark 6. Lightly grease two large baking sheets.

Start by preparing the filling. Melt the butter in a pan, stir in the flour and cook for a minute, then gradually blend in the milk. Bring to the boil, stirring until smooth and thickened. Remove from the heat and season with salt, pepper, nutmeg and mustard. Stir in the cheese until it has melted.

To assemble the puffs, carefully unroll the pastry. Take one sheet and brush over it evenly with melted butter. Cut the pastry into 2½ inch (6 cm) strips. Spoon a little of the sauce on to one corner of the strip of pastry, and fold this corner over to form a triangle. Keep folding the triangle over until the end of the strip is reached and the filling is secured in the centre. Repeat until all the pastry and filling have been used.

Arrange on the baking sheets, brush with more melted butter and bake in the oven for 5 to 10 minutes, until crisp and golden brown. Serve warm.

MAKES about 25 puffs

Cashew Nutters

I must have made thousands of these in my time – so easy, and utterly irresistible too.

PREPARATION AND COOKING TIME: 30 minutes

4 oz (100 g) soft margarine
2 oz (50 g) semolina
3¹/₂ oz (85 g) self-raising flour
3 oz (75 g) well-flavoured Cheddar cheese, grated
salt
¹/₂ level teaspoon dry mustard
freshly ground black pepper
cashew nuts for topping

Heat the oven to 350°F/180°C/Gas Mark 4. Grease a large baking sheet.

Measure all the ingredients except the nuts into a large bowl and work together until thoroughly blended. (This can also be done in a food processor.) Take a large piping bag fitted with a ¹/₂ inch (1.25 cm) plain icing nozzle. Pipe about 40 small blobs on to the baking sheet and press a nut in the centre of each.

Bake in the oven for 15 to 20 minutes until pale golden brown. Cool on a wire rack.

MAKES about 40 nutters

INDEX